The Damnable Heresy of Salvation by Dead Faith

For by grace are ye saved through faith; and that not of yourselves: it is the gift of God: Not of works, lest any man should boast. For we are his workmanship, created in Christ Jesus unto good works, which God hath before ordained that we should walk in them. (Ephesians 2:8-10)

For as the body without the spirit is dead, so faith without works is dead also. (James 2:14, 26)

Edward Hendrie

Copyright © 2021 by Edward Hendrie
ISBN: 978-1-943056-09-5 (Paperback)
ISBN: 978-1-943056-10-1 (Ebook)
EdwardHendrie@gmail.com

Other books from Great Mountain Publishing®
- 9/11-Enemies Foreign and Domestic
- Solving the Mystery of BABYLON THE GREAT
- The Anti-Gospel
- Bloody Zion
- What Shall I Do to Inherit Eternal Life?
- Murder, Rape, and Torture in a Catholic Nunnery
- Antichrist: The Beast Revealed
- The Greatest Lie on Earth
- The Greatest Lie on Earth (Expanded Edition)
- Rome's Responsibility for the Assassination of Abraham Lincoln
- The Sphere of Influence

Available at:
www.antichristconspiracy.com
www.lulu.com
www.911enemies.com
www.mysterybabylonthegreat.net
www.antigospel.com
https://play.google.com
www.barnesandnoble.com
www.amazon.com

Edward Hendrie rests on the authority of the Holy Bible alone for doctrine. He considers the Holy Bible to be the inspired and inerrant word of God. Favorable citation by Edward Hendrie to an authority outside the Holy Bible on a particular issue should not be interpreted to mean that he agrees with all of the doctrines and beliefs of the cited authority. All Scripture references are to the Authorized (King James) Version of the Holy Bible, unless otherwise indicated.

Table of Contents

Introduction 1

1 God-Given Repentance 4

2 James Explains Saving Faith 12

3 The Heresy of Two Justifications 19

4 The Leaven of the Pharisees 28

5 Phinehas Was Justified by God 33

6 The Arminian Apostasy 37

7 Hell Awaits Those Having Faith Without Works 42

8 The Faith of Abraham 47

9 The Free-Will Misinterpretation of John 3:16 64

10 The Faith of Devils 86

11 Easy Believism 95

12 God Has Blinded Their Eyes 102

13 The Malefactor on the Cross 113

14 Running With the Devil 115

15 Loss of Rewards Heresy 121

16 Perfect Salvation 144

17 Two Kinds of Works 149

18	Paul Affirms James	156
19	John and Peter Affirm James and Paul	165
20	The Works of Christ	173
Endnotes		187

Introduction

This book was born out of a controversy over what James means where he says that "Was not Abraham our father justified by works, when he had offered Isaac his son upon the altar?" (James 2:21) Taking that sentence out of context suggests that James is saying that Abraham was justified by works. But James explains his point in the next sentence where he says: "Seest thou how faith wrought with his works, and by works was faith made perfect?" (James 2:22)

James was speaking of his works perfecting his faith. Abraham was justified by faith. Indeed, in the next verse, James explains that very fact: "And the scripture was fulfilled which saith, Abraham believed God, and it was imputed unto him for righteousness: and he was called the Friend of God." (James 2:23)

James reiterates that Abraham was justified by faith according to the scriptures. "Abraham believed God, and it was imputed unto him for righteousness." But then, what does James do after clarifying his point, he goes right back to saying: "Ye see then how that by works a man is justified, and not by faith only." (James 2:24) Again, James drives home the interplay of faith and works. He concludes with his main point: "For as the body without the spirit is dead, so faith without works is dead also." (James 2:26)

James is every bit part of the gospel as any other book in

the Bible. The teaching of James is that faith without works is dead faith. That means that such dead faith is not saving faith. James explains: "What doth it profit, my brethren, though a man say he hath faith, and have not works? can faith save him?" (James 2:14) The answer is no. Faith without works cannot save a person.

James explains that faith that has no fruit is dead faith. James calls such dead faith, the faith of devils.

> Thou believest that there is one God; thou doest well: the devils also believe, and tremble. But wilt thou know, O vain man, that faith without works is dead? (James 2:19-20)

James is not saying that salvation is by works. He confirmed the gospel message that true faith comes with good works. As Paul explained:

> For by grace are ye saved through faith; and that not of yourselves: it is the gift of God: Not of works, lest any man should boast. For we are his workmanship, created in Christ Jesus unto **good works**, which God hath before ordained that we should walk in them. (Ephesians 2:8-10)

We are saved by the grace of God through faith in Jesus Christ to bear fruit. The fruit does not save us. No works can save us. We are saved by faith. But saving faith will bear fruit. God has ordained that his elect bear fruit. If you are saved, you will bear fruit because God has willed it. "Ye have not chosen me, but I have chosen you, and **ordained you, that ye should go and bring forth fruit**, and that your fruit should remain: that whatsoever ye shall ask of the Father in my name, he may give it you." (John 15:16)

Jesus states that by bearing the fruit of salvation, God is

glorified. Furthermore, bearing fruit is what his elect will do. Jesus said that by bearing the fruit of salvation, "so shall ye be my disciples."

> Herein is my Father glorified, that ye bear much fruit; **so shall ye be my disciples**. (John 15:8)

Fruit is God's stamp of approval. Thus, the contrary is true. Just as James pointed out, if one is NOT bearing fruit that means that person is NOT a disciple of Jesus Christ.

Despite the clear theme in the Bible that true faith bears fruit, there are heretical preachers promoting a false gospel of salvation by dead faith.

1 God-Given Repentance

God calls believers to repentance. "Bring forth therefore fruits meet for repentance:" Matthew 3:8. *See also* Acts 26:20. Indeed, the Bible is clear that salvation brings repentance. Repentance is the flip side of faith. Once God moves a person to be born again, he is freed from sin and turns toward God in faith.

> Therefore if any man be in Christ, he is a new creature: old things are passed away; behold, all things are become new. (2 Corinthians 5:17)

The turning toward God involves a turning away from the former sin. While faith is not a work, repentance is manifested through works. Faith is also manifested in works. "Faith without works is dead." James 2:20. Faith is a gift of God. Ephesians 2:8, Galatians 3:22. If faith comes from God, then so does repentance. God leads us to repentance.

> Or despisest thou the riches of his goodness and forbearance and longsuffering; not knowing that **the goodness of God <u>leadeth</u> thee to repentance**? (Romans 2:4)

A person whose heart God hardens (Matthew 13:11-16; Exodus 14:4) cannot repent. Such are reserved for destruction. "But after thy hardness and **impenitent heart** treasurest up unto thyself wrath against the day of wrath and revelation of the righteous judgment of God;" (Romans 2:5) Such will be judged according to their evil deeds. Romans 2:6.

Repentance, which is the turning from sin toward God is accomplished by God.

> **Turn us, O God of our salvation**, and cause thine anger toward us to cease. (Psalms 85:4)

Man does not, indeed he cannot, repent of his sin on his own, because his will is enslaved to sin. Repentance is entirely of God. God changes the hearts of his elect and turns them to repent of their sins. "Unto you first God, having raised up his Son Jesus, sent him to bless you, **in turning away every one of you from his iniquities**." (Acts 3:26)

Turning toward God is not a free-will decision. If it were, that means that the turning away from sin is also a free-will decision. That, however, is not what God says. God reveals in the book of Acts that it is God who "grants" repentance.

> When they heard these things, they held their peace, and glorified God, saying, Then hath **God also to the Gentiles <u>granted</u> repentance unto life**. (Acts 11:18)

The fact that repentance comes from God and not from the free will of man was clearly understood by the early church. We see the writer of 2 Timothy expressing God's sovereign rule over the hearts of men; God "gives" repentance.

And the servant of the Lord must not strive; but be

> gentle unto all men, apt to teach, patient, In meekness instructing those that oppose themselves; **if God peradventure will <u>give</u> them repentance to the acknowledging of the truth**. (2 Timothy 2:24-25)

Without God moving the heart of the penitent, there could never be repentance. It is Jesus that supplies the faith and the repentance.

> Him hath God exalted with his right hand to be a Prince and a Saviour, for **to give repentance to Israel**, and forgiveness of sins. (Acts 5:31)

Repentance is manifested by works. If repentance is by the free will of man, that means that those works are born of man's free will. Such a theology constitutes salvation by works.

Read what the book of Acts states about the relationship of repentance to salvation.

> Therefore let all the house of Israel know assuredly, that God hath made that same Jesus, whom ye have crucified, both Lord and Christ. Now when they heard this, they were pricked in their heart, and said unto Peter and to the rest of the apostles, Men *and* brethren, what shall we do? Then Peter said unto them, **Repent**, and be baptized every one of you in the name of Jesus Christ for the remission of sins, and ye shall receive the gift of the Holy Ghost. (Acts 2:36-38)

Notice that when the people heard Peter preach the gospel "they were pricked in their heart." That was God effectually drawing them to Christ. They then asked Peter "what shall we do?" Peter told them to "repent, and be baptized." Repentance in the biblical context means to change one's mind and stop sinning; to turn away from sin and toward Christ. If the people could repent of their own free will that would make Peter's command to repent a command to work their way to salvation.

The gospel, however, states that the spiritual rebirth is entirely the work of the Holy Spirit. That means that repentance is a fruit of the Spirit, which is also accomplished by God. It is not a work of the free will of man at all. The gospel is salvation by grace through faith, with repentance from sin being the fruit of the true faith of Jesus Christ. Peter's command to the people to repent and be baptized was not a command to work toward heaven because they could not repent unless God gave then the faith of Jesus to turn toward him in faith. Paul told King Agrippa how he preached the gospel to the Gentiles. Paul stated that Jesus told him:

> But rise, and stand upon thy feet: for I have appeared unto thee for this purpose, to make thee a minister and a witness both of these things which thou hast seen, and of those things in the which I will appear unto thee; Delivering thee from the people, and from the Gentiles, unto whom now I send thee, To open their eyes, and to turn them from darkness to light, and from the power of Satan unto God, that they may receive forgiveness of sins, and inheritance among them which are sanctified by faith that is in me. Whereupon, O king Agrippa, I was not disobedient unto the heavenly vision: But shewed first unto them of Damascus, and at Jerusalem, and throughout all the coasts of Judaea, and then to the Gentiles, that **they should repent and turn to God, and do works meet for repentance**." (Acts 26:16-20)

Jesus commanded Paul to go to the Gentiles and "open

their eyes, and turn them from darkness to light, and from the power of Satan unto God, that they may receive forgiveness of sins, and inheritance among them which are sanctified by faith that is in me." Paul's mission was to preach the gospel to the Gentiles. What did Paul tell the Gentiles to do? Paul told the Gentiles to repent of their sin and "do works meet for repentance." If repentance is a fruit of the Spirit that is born by the faith of Jesus Christ, then Paul's admonition was in complete accord with the gospel. If repentance is an act of the free will of man, then Paul was all wrong in his approach. If repentance is a free will act, then Paul was preaching a false gospel of works by telling them to "do works meet for repentance."

Notice that in the letter to the Thessalonians, Paul revealed their repentance in turning from idols toward Christ. This repentance was accomplished by God. "For they themselves shew of us what manner of entering in we had unto you, and how ye turned to God from idols to serve the living and true God;" (1 Thessalonians 1:9)

God reveals in 2 Peter 3:9 that repentance is what saves a person from perishing in hell. Peter states:

> The Lord is not slack concerning his promise, as some men count slackness; but is longsuffering to us-ward, **not willing that any should perish, but that all should come to repentance**. 2 Peter 3:9.

Incidentally, many apostate preachers claim that passage means that God is not willing that anyone in the world will perish. They claim that passage proves that salvation is by the free-will choice of man and God is impotently wringing his hands in the hope that people will believe in him.

The unbiblical doctrine that God is willing that all should be saved, and that it is only man's free will that thwarts God's desires, has crept into many ostensibly Protestant churches. These corrupted churches point to part of 2 Peter 3:9 taken out of context as authority for their doctrine. In fact, this single passage is so key to the Arminian theology that it is the motto of the *Society of Evangelical Arminians*:[1] **"Not Willing That Any Should Perish."** That clause is being taken out of context from 2 Peter 3:9.

The Arminians have hijacked the gospel and all of the terms that have traditionally been used in the Christian community to describe orthodox biblical Christianity. An organization calling itself the *Society of Evangelical Arminians* makes no historical sense. While almost all Arminians consider themselves evangelicals, they deny the foundational biblical doctrines that are at the core of what it historically meant to be an evangelical. Dr. Michael Scott Horton, who is the J. Gresham Machen Professor of Systematic Theology and Apologetics, in his article *Evangelical Arminians, Option or Oxymoron?*, explains that it is an oxymoron for an Arminian to be described as an evangelical.

> T]he evangelicals who faced this challenge of Arminianism universally regarded it as a heretical departure from the Christian faith. One simply could not deny total depravity, unconditional election, justification by grace alone through faith alone because of Christ alone, and continue to call himself or herself an evangelical. There were many Christians who were not evangelicals, but to be an evangelical meant that one adhered to these biblical convictions. ... Today one can be an evangelical-which has historically meant holding to total depravity, unconditional election, justification by grace through faith alone, the sufficiency of scripture-and at the same time be an Arminian, denying or distorting this very evangelical message.[2]

Franklin Graham, son of Billy Graham, speaking on behalf of the Billy Graham Evangelistic Association, stated: "According to 2 Peter 3:9, the Lord is 'not willing that any should perish but that all should come to repentance.'"[3]

At first glance it would appear that 2 Peter 3:9 supports what Graham has said. Closer examination of that passage reveals that the passage does not in fact support that false Arminian free-will doctrine promoted by Graham. Notice the missing passage. "The Lord is [...] not willing that any should perish, but that all should come to repentance." 2 Peter 3:9.

Those who try to force the square peg of scripture into the round hole of their false doctrine must shave off parts of the Bible in order to get it to fit. In this case, Graham, as is the practice with all Arminians, shaved that portion of the passage which limits its application to those who are already chosen for salvation. What God means in that passage is that God is not willing that any who have been chosen for salvation should perish, but that all those who are saved should come to repentance. Read the entire passage in context and you will see that God is "longsuffering to us-ward." God is not willing that "us" should perish and that "us" should come to repentance.

> The Lord is not slack concerning his promise, as some men count slackness; but is **longsuffering to us-ward,** not willing that any should perish, but that all should come to repentance. 2 Peter 3:9.

Who are the "us" in 2 Peter 3:9? Simply read the first paragraph of the letter and we see that Peter is writing to "them that have obtained like precious faith with us." "Simon Peter, a servant and an apostle of Jesus Christ, to them that have obtained like precious faith with us through the righteousness of God and our Saviour Jesus Christ:" (2 Peter 1:1)

One can see that in 2 Peter 3:9, Peter was stating that God was not willing that any who believe in Jesus should perish. God's will is always done, and his will cannot be thwarted by man's will. If God has foreordained one to salvation, no one can stay his hand. "And all the inhabitants of the earth are reputed as nothing: and he doeth according to his will in the army of heaven, and among the inhabitants of the earth: and none can stay his hand, or say unto him, What doest thou?" (Daniel 4:35)

2 James Explains Saving Faith

Repentance and faith go hand in hand. Without works, faith is dead. That is what James meant when he said: "Even so faith, if it hath not works, is dead, being alone." (James 2:17) If faith is from the free will of man as falsely claimed by most preachers, and given that faith without works is dead, under that free-will heresy, salvation must necessarily be by the free will works of man. Because under the Arminianism free-will heresy, man can lose his salvation because he is supposedly able to change his mind, the Armininian believer must be kept on his toes to work, work, work his way to heaven lest he be found lacking.

A true Christian, on the other hand, will manifest his faith by his works. The works, however, do not merit salvation. The faith of the elect is from God and so are their works. The works are prepared by God ahead of time for his elect to walk in them. Ephesians 2:10. James explained:

> Was not **Abraham** our father **justified by works**, when he had **offered Isaac** his son upon the altar? Seest thou how faith wrought with his works, and by works was faith made perfect? (James 2:21-22)

While a true believer will have good works as a necessary fruit of their salvation, the contrary is true also. A person who does not have the fruit of good works does not have saving faith. James repeatedly states that "faith without works is dead." He means by that statement that such faith is not saving faith.

> **What doth it profit, my brethren, though a man say he hath faith, and have not works? can faith save him?** (James 2:14)

Indeed, James describes faith that has no works as the faith of devils.

> Thou believest that there is one God; thou doest well: **the devils also believe, and tremble**. But wilt thou know, O vain man, that **faith without works is dead**? (James 2:19-20)

James states that works that are born of repentance are necessary fruits of saving faith. He even cites the very example of Abraham. Repentance is the flip side of faith and is manifested by works. Notice that in Hebrews 11:17, Paul states that Abraham offered up Isaac by "faith," yet James states that Abraham was "justified by works" when he offered Isaac as a sacrifice.

> **By faith Abraham**, when he was tried, **offered up Isaac**: and he that had received the promises offered up his only begotten son," (Hebrews 11:17)

James drives the point home that faith without works is not saving faith. Abraham's faith was perfect faith since it was manifested by his works. **"Seest thou how faith wrought with his** [Abraham's] **works, and by works was faith made perfect?"** (James 2:22)

This same parallelism is seen with Rahab. James states

that she was justified by works (meaning that her faith was true faith that was manifested by works).

> Likewise also was not **Rahab** the harlot **justified by works**, when she had received the messengers, and had sent them out another way? (James 2:25)

However, that same Rahab was given as an example of faith in the letter to Hebrews.

> **By faith** the harlot **Rahab** perished not with them that believed not, when she had received the spies with peace. (Hebrews 11:31)

We are saved to bear fruit. God has ordained that his elect bear fruit. If you are saved, you will bear fruit because God has willed it. "Ye have not chosen me, but I have chosen you, and **ordained you, that ye should go and bring forth fruit**, and that your fruit should remain: that whatsoever ye shall ask of the Father in my name, he may give it you." (John 15:16)

Jesus states God is glorified when we bear the fruit of salvation. Furthermore, bearing fruit is what his elect will do. Jesus said that by bearing the fruit of salvation, "so shall ye be my disciples."

> Herein is my Father glorified, that ye bear much fruit; so shall ye be my disciples. (John 15:8)

Fruit is God's stamp of approval. Thus, the contrary is true. Just as James pointed out, if one is not bearing fruit that means that person is NOT a disciple of Jesus Christ.

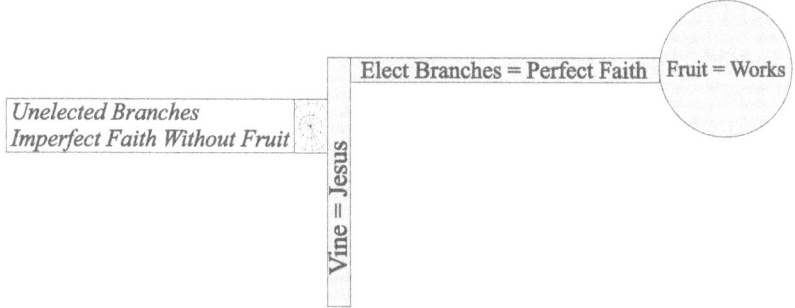

"Every branch in me that beareth not fruit he taketh away: and every branch that beareth fruit, he purgeth it, that it may bring forth more fruit. ... I am the vine, ye are the branches: He that abideth in me, and I in him, the same bringeth forth much fruit: for without me ye can do nothing. **If a man abide not in me, he is cast forth as a branch, and is withered; and men gather them, and cast them into the fire, and they are burned.** ... **Herein is my Father glorified, that ye bear much fruit; so shall ye be my disciples.**" (John 15:2, 5-6, 8)

The fruit to which Jesus speaks will be manifested in the good works that spring from the new charitable heart God has given those who believe. Faith without works is dead!

> **Even so faith, if it hath not works, is dead**, being alone. Yea, a man may say, Thou hast faith, and I have works: shew me thy faith without thy works, and I will shew thee my faith by my works. Thou believest that there is one God; thou doest well: the devils also believe, and tremble. But wilt thou know, O vain man, **that faith without works is dead**? (James 2:17-20)

James explains at the outset of his letter: "But be ye doers of the word, and not hearers only, deceiving your own selves." (James 1:22) James summarizes what he means: "If ye fulfil the royal law according to the scripture, Thou shalt love thy neighbour as thyself, ye do well." (James 2:8) Our fruit is born of faith; that fruit is love toward others. What did Paul say? He said: "And now abideth faith, hope, charity, these three; but the greatest of these is charity." 1 Corinthians 13:13. Why did he say that charity was greater than faith? Because without charity, faith is dead.

God prunes us so that we will bear fruit: "Every branch in me that beareth not fruit he taketh away: and every branch that beareth fruit, he purgeth it, that it may bring forth more fruit." (John 15:2) If a branch does not bear fruit, it is good for nothing but destruction.

Jesus stated any fruit comes from him and that without him man can bear no fruit. "I am the vine, ye are the branches: He that abideth in me, and I in him, the same bringeth forth much fruit: for **without me ye can do nothing."** (John 15:5)

There can be no faith without repentance; all repentance brings forth fruit. The Bible states that all faith, repentance, and fruit are from God. They all go together. The free-will Arminian theology has faith and repentance and fruit, but they all come from man. The fruit of faith and repentance is good works. Since the Arminian believer is the source of the good works, Arminianism constitutes salvation by works.

The Arminian model of repentance is explained in the Arminian Confession of 1621, which was drafted by Simon Episcopius (A/K/A Simon Bisschop), protégé of Jacobus Arminius, and one of the principal Arminian Remonstrants. Arminianism requires that repentance be effectual, sincere, and continual.[4] The Arminian repentance requires the free will exercise of good works. Repentance "must always outwardly exert itself through acts of virtue, as often as there is occasion and can be done."[5]

That Arminian free-will view is heresy. Just as faith without works is dead, so also works from the free-will of man are just as dead. The works spoken of by James are not the works of the flesh; they are the works of God done through man. God is watching our every step. "For the ways of man are before the eyes of the LORD, and he pondereth all his goings." (Proverbs 5:21) Not only is God watching our every step; he is ordering those steps. "The steps of a good man are ordered by the Lord: and he delighteth in his way." Psalm 37:23. A man may think that he is ordering his own steps, but he is not. "O LORD, I know that the way of man is not in himself: it is not in man that walketh to direct his steps." (Jeremiah 10:23) Man may devise his way, but man does not direct his own steps, God does that. "A man's heart deviseth his way: but the Lord directeth his steps." Proverbs 16:9. Other than by revelation in the Bible, man would not know that God is directing his steps. "Man's goings are of the LORD; how can a man then understand his own way?" (Proverbs 20:24) God's elect are spiritual creations of God for the purpose of walking in good works. Those good works are prepared by God in advance for us to perform. In Ephesians 2, God states that Christians are saved by his grace through faith in Jesus Christ and are pre-ordained and born again as his workmanship to walk in good works.

> For by grace are ye saved through faith; and that not of yourselves: it is the gift of God: Not of works, lest any man should boast. For we are his workmanship, created in Christ Jesus unto good works, which God hath before ordained that we should walk in them. (Ephesians 2:8-10)

If his will is that we will do good works, then we will do good works. God's his will is done on earth just as his will is done in heaven. "Thy kingdom come. Thy will be done in earth, as it is in heaven." (Matthew 6:10) God acts in accordance with his will, and no one can stay the hand of God!

> And all the inhabitants of the earth are reputed as nothing: and he doeth according to his will in the army of heaven, and among the inhabitants of the earth: and none can stay his hand, or say unto him, What doest thou? (Daniel 4:35)

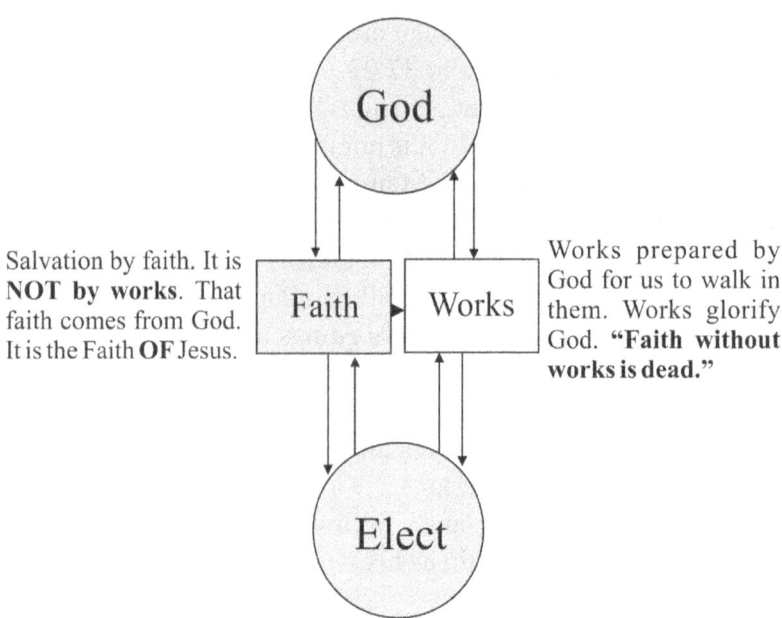

"For by grace are ye **saved through faith**; and that not of yourselves: it is the gift of God: **Not of works**, lest any man should boast. **For we are his workmanship, created in Christ Jesus unto good works, which God hath before ordained that we should walk in them."** Ephesians 2:8-10. Thus, faith is from God. It is the faith **OF** Jesus. Romans 3:22. Jesus is the author and finisher of our faith. Hebrews 12:2. **"Faith without works is dead."** James 2:20. All disciples of Christ will bear fruit of salvation, and that fruit glorifies God. John 15:8.

3 The Heresy of Two Justifications

James, Chapter 2 has been a fly in the ointment for many theologians who do not understand the gospel. They seek to create their own Christian theology without regard to what God has actually said. And James, Chapter 2, threatens their corrupt vision of the gospel. James, Chapter 2 vexed even the esteemed Martin Luther. He railed against it and proposed that it be stricken from the Bible. Shawn Lazar, writing for *Grace in Focus* reveals:

> Martin Luther was so vexed by this passage that he not only called the letter of James "an epistle of straw" (LW 35, 362), he also proposed it must have been written by "some Jew" who "probably heard about Christian people but never encountered any" and urged his students to "throw the epistle of James out of this school [i.e., Wittenberg], for it doesn't amount to much" (LW 54, 424)![6]

Zane Hodges (1932-2008) was a highly respected Bible scholar. He was Professor of New Testament Greek and Exegesis at Dallas Theological Seminary for 27 years, pastor at Victor Street Bible Chapel for more than 50 years, and the author of numerous books.[7] Zane Hodges explains in his book, The Epistle of James[8], that there are two justifications in the Bible. "When, however, one is justified by works, he or she achieves an intimacy with God that is manifest to others."[9]

Hodges cannot allow that James is speaking to the justification by God, and so he conjures up two justifications. Hodges alleges:

> James is saying that a by-faith justification is not the only kind of justification there is. There is also a by-works justification. The former type is before God, the latter type is before men.[10]

Hodges elaborates that when James spoke of the justification of Rahab by works he was speaking of justification before men and NOT before God.

> Rahab, like Abraham before her, was justified by works in front of other people, that is, before the nation of Israel among whom she came to live.[11]

Shawn Lazar borrows from Hodges and elaborates on the theme of two justifications. Lazar explains, as did Hodges, that James' epistle was not talking about justification before God, but rather James was talking about justification before men. He distinguished the justification preached by Paul from the justification preached by James. He alleged that Paul preached a justification by God, whereas James preached a different kind of justification, which is justification before men. Lazar states:

> First, Paul and James use different terminology. Paul wrote about "justification by faith" (Gal 2:16, Rom 3:28), while James wrote about "justification

by works" (Jas 2:21, 24). Why would anyone think they were talking about the same thing? If there were two cans in your grandmother's pantry, one labelled "Peaches" and the other labelled "Plums," would you assume each can contained a mixture of peaches and plums? Of course not. So why do it here? A plain reading of their differing terminology suggests that **Paul and James were talking about two different kinds of justification.**[12]

Lazar explains that he viewed that there is justification by God and a different justification before men. Lazar opines that the justification before God is by faith, but the justification before men is by works.

But then in Rom 4:2, Paul implies there is a second kind of justification, one that is by works, and which is not before God. Who is it before? Evidently, it's before men. That's the kind of justification James is talking about in 2:14-26, one that is by works and before other people. When Abraham offered up Isaac, his faith was vindicated (i.e., justified) before men, and he became known far and wide as "the friend of God" (Jas 2:23). Likewise, Rahab was vindicated before all Israel when she hid the spies and sent them away safely. Her actions proved to Israel that she believed in their God. **She was justified by her works before men.**[13]

We can find the thread of this two justifications heresy in one form or another in the writings of respected Bible scholars. For example, John Gill (1697-1771) writes:

Moreover, the Apostle Paul speaks of justification

> before God; and James speaks of it as it is known by its fruits unto men; the one speaks of a justification of their persons, in the sight of God; the other of the justification and approbation of their cause, their conduct, and their faith before men.[14]

Dr. John MacArthur is the pastor of Grace Community Church in Sun Valley, California, and president of The Master's College and Seminary. MacArthur has written over 100 books, which have sold millions worldwide. He had this to say about the two justifications that he alleges are found in the gospel.

> What does James me when it says here in James, was not Abraham our Father justified by works. Listen to this; **Abraham was justified by faith before God but he was justified by works before men.** You see the difference. That's the whole point James is making. Works are the only way his faith can be seen and verified as real saving faith by himself or any other man. The only way I can know I'm genuinely redeemed is to see the pattern of my godliness, the evidence. The only way you can know it is to see my life and it is this justification before men that James has in mind. Paul was emphasizing justification before God. James is emphasizing the vindication of a man's claim to salvation before others.[15]

MacArthur's error is based upon a misinterpretation of Paul's writings found in Romans 4:2, which states: "For if Abraham were justified by works, he hath whereof to glory; but not before God." (Romans 4:2) The argument made by MacArthur is that since Abraham cannot be justified before God by works, he can be justified before men by works. Where does he come up with that conclusion? He takes James 2:21 out of context. That passage states: "Was not Abraham our father justified by works, when he had offered Isaac his son upon the altar?" (James 2:21)

MacArthur argues that since Paul said that Abraham could not be justified before God by works, he must be justified before men by works. He says that because James said Abraham was justified by works, and therefore because those works could not justify Abraham before God, they could only justify Abraham before men.

There are some significant problems with that construct. First, Paul says Abraham was not justified by works before God. But that does not mean that Paul was conveying that Abraham was justified before men. Paul never said that. James said that Abraham was justified by works, and that also does not mean that Abraham was justified before men.

James meant that Abraham was justified by faith before God, and that justifying faith was manifested by his works. We can read what he said in context.

> Was not Abraham our father justified by works, when he had offered Isaac his son upon the altar? Seest thou how faith wrought with his works, and by works was faith made perfect? And the scripture was fulfilled which saith, Abraham believed God, and it was imputed unto him for righteousness: and he was called the Friend of God. (James 2:21-23)

Notice that immediately after James said that Abraham was justified by works, he explained that Abraham's "faith wrought with his works, and by works was faith made perfect." James was speaking to the perfect faith of Abraham that was manifested in his works. And he drives the point home that salvation is by faith when in the next sequential verse he states that "Abraham believed

God, and it was imputed unto him for righteousness."

James says Abraham was "justified by works;" meaning that "by works was [Abraham's] faith made perfect;" which means that Abraham was justified by perfect faith bearing the fruit thereof because "Abraham believed God, and it was imputed unto him for righteousness."

The justification in James was justification by God and not before men. That justification was by faith, which was made perfect by works prepared by God for Abraham to walk in them.

This error interpreting James, Chapter 2 as speaking of Justification before men is endemic in the "Christian" church today. Don Fortner (1950-2020), former pastor of Grace Baptist Church of Danville, Kentucky states that James, Chapter 2, means that "[e]very true believer is justified before men by the display of good works."[16] Fortner pontificates further:

> [A]ll who know Christ, in the experience of grace, are justified by the display of good works before men (James 2:14-26). Yes, there is a sense in which we are justified by works, not before God, but before men. We justify our profession of faith in Christ by our works. Believers do not show their faith by creeds, confessions, and catechisms, but by their conduct. This is what the Holy Spirit teaches us in James 2:14-26.

It seems that the erroneous belief that James is discussing the justification of believers before men spans the theological spectrum. John MacArthur and Don Fortner accept the sovereign grace of God in electing believers, whereas Steven Anderson is a staunch Arminian who denies the sovereign election by God of believers. Indeed, Anderson is on record saying that he hates the doctrine of the sovereign election of God (which he pejoratively calls Calvinism).[17]

It is not surprising that Anderson, being an enemy of the gospel, views James, chapter 2, to mean justification before men and NOT God. Anderson preaches the following about James, Chapter 2:

> Now you see in what way a man is justified by works. And what is that way? **Before man, not before God. Now you see how a man is justified by works. It's not before God. It's not salvation**. … We're talking to the saved. We're talking to believers. And when he talks to believers here's what he says to them, he's telling the believers, you need to get some works to go with your faith. Now listen if faith just automatically produced works, he wouldn't even have to say that because it would be automatic. It doesn't make sense. They're missing the whole point of the passage. The whole point of the passage is to show your faith by your works, and not to just sit around oh I have faith. Do the work.[18]

Notice that he is saying that Christians are justified before men and NOT God. He then segues to his claim that James is admonishing: "you need to get some works to go with your faith." The problem with that is that the only way that one could be justified before men would be if the person did the works to be seen of men. The admonition that "you need to get some works to go with your faith," is an admonition to do works to be seen of men to be justified before those men.

Because Anderson is a free-will Arminian, he believes that both faith and works flow from man's free-will and are not gifts from God. That is why he also preaches the false doctrine that "you don't need to repent of your sins to be saved."[19] But the gospel preached by Paul was for the people to repent and do works of that repentance.

> But shewed first unto them of Damascus, and at Jerusalem, and throughout all the coasts of Judaea, and then to the Gentiles, that they should repent and turn to God, and do works meet for repentance. (Acts 26:20)

Paul preached repentance because Jesus Christ instructed Paul to do that. Jesus told Paul to "turn them from darkness to light." That means to bring them to repentance.

> To open their eyes, and to **turn them from darkness to light**, and from the power of Satan unto God, that they may receive forgiveness of sins, and inheritance among them which are sanctified by faith that is in me." (Acts 26:18)

Peter preached the gospel of repentance unto salvation. "**Repent** ye therefore, and be converted, that your sins may be blotted out, when the times of refreshing shall come from the presence of the Lord;" (Acts 3:19) God "now commandeth all men every where to **repent**." (Acts 17:30) Paul testified "both to the Jews, and also to the Greeks, **repentance** toward God, and faith toward our Lord Jesus Christ." (Acts 20:21)

We are called on to repent of the former things and not live after the flesh but mortify the deeds of the flesh and live by faith. This is something that only God can do for us. That is why Paul explains that "as many as are led by the Spirit of God, they are the sons of God."

> "Therefore, brethren, we are debtors, not to the flesh, to live after the flesh. For if ye live after the flesh, ye shall die: but if ye through the Spirit do

mortify the deeds of the body, ye shall live. For as many as are led by the Spirit of God, they are the sons of God." (Romans 8:12-14)

Jesus explained: "I came not to call the righteous, but sinners to **repentance**." (Luke 5:32) He called on his disciples to preach repentance to all nations. "And that **repentance** and remission of sins should be preached in his name among all nations, beginning at Jerusalem." (Luke 24:47)

Recall in Acts 2:37 the people "were pricked in their heart" after hearing the gospel. That was God effectually drawing them to Christ. After being pricked in the heart, they asked Peter "what shall we do?" In Acts 2:38 we read that Peter told them to "repent, and be baptized." Repentance in the biblical context means to change one's mind and stop sinning, to turn away from sin and toward Christ. If the people could repent of their own free will that would make Peter's command to repent a command to work their way to salvation. But Peter understood that repentance is the work of God.

Steven Anderson does not understand the truth that both faith and repentance are gifts from God. He thinks that both faith and repentance are by the free-will of man. Consequently, Anderson views the requirement of repentance for justification as being salvation by works. It is not. There can be no faith without repentance. The elect turn toward Christ in Faith and away from sin in repentance. Faith and repentance go together. Faith is of God. The repentance that comes with faith is from God. And the fruit of that faith and repentance is from God. That is the grace of God.

4 The Leaven of the Pharisees

Those who preach that James is advocating justification by works before men are preaching the leaven of the Pharisees. Jesus warned us about that in Mathew 16:6. What is that leaven? Jesus explained in Matthew 16:12 that the leaven of the Pharisees was their doctrine. In Matthew 23:28, Jesus revealed how their doctrine caused the Pharisees to be puffed up and seek to outwardly appear to be righteous before men. "Even so ye also outwardly appear righteous unto men, but within ye are full of hypocrisy and iniquity." (Matthew 23:28) The Pharisees loved to be justified before men. God calls such justification before men an abomination in God's sight.

> And he said unto them, Ye are they which justify yourselves before men; but God knoweth your hearts: for that which is highly esteemed among men is **abomination in the sight of God.**" (Luke 16:15)

Preaching that a Christian's works justify him before men is to preach what God describes as an "abomination in the sight of God." Luke 16:15.

Adding insult to injury, such preaching violates the

command of God in Matthew 6.1 to do our alms in secret. Indeed, if we obeyed God's command to do our good works in secret, then it would be impossible to be justified by men as advocated by Anderson.

> **Take heed that ye do not your alms before men, to be seen of them**: otherwise ye have no reward of your Father which is in heaven. Therefore when thou doest thine alms, do not sound a trumpet before thee, as the hypocrites do in the synagogues and in the streets, that they may have glory of men. Verily I say unto you, They have their reward. But when thou doest alms, let not thy left hand know what thy right hand doeth: That thine alms may be in secret: and thy Father which seeth in secret himself shall reward thee openly. Matthew 6:1-4.

Justification has a particular meaning throughout the Bible. It means to be made righteous in the sight of God. Justification is something done by God, not by man. Only God can justify. There can be no biblical justification before men. To teach that James was saying that we are justified (made perfectly righteous) before men is heresy. ONLY God can justify you.

Preachers who claim that James was advocating justification before men and NOT by God do not understand what justification means. They think that our works only justify us in the sight of men. They create a contrivance of two justifications: one justification before God, and another justification before men. But the two justifications is an unbliblcal contrivance. There is only one justification in the Bible, and that justification is by God. It is God that Justifies.

Only God can justify a man. "Who shall lay any thing to the charge of God's elect? **It is God that justifieth."** (Romans 8:33) And only works done by God are righteous. God works through his elect to do the works of righteousness. "For it is God which worketh in you both to will and to do of his good pleasure." Philippians 2:13. God sees all the righteous works done by his elect. "[T]he eyes of the Lord are over the righteous." 1 Peter 3:12.

Justification before men is a false justification. And to preach such a thing is to implant in the minds of men that our good works justify us before men. The only way to ensure that our good works can justify us before men would be if a person goes out of his way to violate God's command in Matthew 6:1 and do the good works to be seen of men. That is what the Pharisees did. It is the leaven (doctrine) of the Pharisees that Jesus warned us about in Matthew 16:6-12. Jesus said that for the Pharisees to justify themselves before men was an "abomination in the sight of God." (Luke 16:15)

To teach that our works justify us in the sight of men is unscriptural. Such teaching only motivates people to display their works to the world to be justified by men. It violates God's command in Matthew 6:1 to do our alms in secret. Indeed, if we obeyed God's command to do our good works in secret, then it would be impossible to be justified by men. To teach that James meant justification before men in James 2:21, 24, and 25 is heresy. It is especially heretical to teach that James' reference to justification in 2:21, 24, and 25 does NOT mean justification by God.

God said in James that faith without works is dead.

For as the body without the spirit is dead, so **faith without works is dead** also. (James 2:26)

Paul makes it clear that we are saved by grace through faith and not of works. But we are born again as new creations to do good works prepared ahead of time by God to walk in them.

> For by grace are ye saved through faith; and that not of yourselves: [it is] the gift of God: Not of works, lest any man should boast. For we are his workmanship, created in Christ Jesus unto good works, which God hath before ordained that we should walk in them. (Ephesians 2:8-10)

There is a reason. Our good works are actually the works of God done through us. Once God saves us, we will bear fruit of that salvation.

> Herein is my Father glorified, that ye bear much fruit; so shall ye be my disciples. (John 15:8)

That is the gospel. The justification by works before men crowd do not understand the gospel. They claim that the justification by faith with works discussed in James, Chapter 2, is ONLY a reference to justification by faith with works before men and NOT a reference to justification by faith with works by God. Their theology is heresy, and it is the doctrine of the Pharisees. Jesus upbraided the Pharisees for just such a doctrine: "Ye are they which justify yourselves before men." Luke 16:15.

For man to declare someone justified for wickedness is an abomination to the Lord. "He that justifieth the wicked, and he that condemneth the just, even they both are abomination to the LORD." Proverbs 17:15. Justification in Proverbs 17:15 is similar to the justification provided for by God, in the sense that it is a declaration of justification and not an impartation of actual righteousness. It is the epitome of evil for man to justify the wicked by declaring them not guilty for their wickedness. That is because a declaration by man that the wicked is justified is, by definition, an injustice. Even if the sinner were to be punished for his wickedness, he could not be justified because he is still guilty of the wicked act. Being punished does not justify the act and render him not guilty.

While it is the epitome of unrighteousness for man to justify the wicked, it is the epitome of righteousness for God to do that same thing. That is because God justifies the wicked through the atonement of his Holy Son, Jesus Christ. If God were to punish the sinner directly, the sinner would be punished, but he could never be justified, because the guilt for the sin would remain. The only way to justify the sinner is by having Jesus trade places with the sinner. There was a perfect legal exchange at the cross, which accomplished justification. The righteousness of Jesus is imputed to the sinner, and the sins of the sinner are imputed to Jesus.

Without the imputation of the righteousness of Christ to the sinner, justification of the sinner would be an abomination. That is why Jesus had to atone for the sins of his elect. It is only through the grace of God by faith in Jesus Christ that man can be justified. The sacrifice of Jesus accomplished the justification of the wicked because God sees only the righteousness of Christ when he sees a believer. The believer is thus justified in God's eyes. The believer only needs to believe in Jesus. His faith in Jesus will justify him before God. Notice in the parallel passages below that justification is by grace and also by faith. Faith and grace go hand in hand, which indicates that faith is provided by God through his sovereign grace.

> Being **justified freely by his grace** through the redemption that is in Christ Jesus: Romans 3:24
>
> Therefore being **justified by faith**, we have peace with God through our Lord Jesus Christ. Romans 5:1.
>
> That being **justified by his grace**, we should be made heirs according to the hope of eternal life. Titus 3:7.

5 Phinehas Was Justified by God

Some have cited Psalms 106 to support the claim that James 2 is speaking of works justifying men in the sight of others because they allege that Phinehas was justified before men in Palms 106:31.[20] Psalms 106:31 does not support the claim that James was advocating that a Christian is Justified before men because Psalm 106:31 reveals that God justified Phinehas.

> Then stood up Phinehas, and executed judgment: and so the plague was stayed. And that was counted unto him for righteousness unto all generations for evermore. Psalms 106:30-31.

The psalmist wrote the words given to him by revelation from God. It is God speaking through the psalmist. The psalmist could not, himself, declare that Phinehas was justified; only God could do that. And God revealed to the psalmist that God justified Phinehas. What Phinehas did "was counted unto him for righteousness unto all generations for evermore." While the psalmist was the writer, he was only the instrument in God's hands, revealing God's words.

Who was it that counted what Phinehas did as

righteousness unto all generations? It was God (NOT man); just as God accounted Abraham's faith (manifested by his works) for righteousness as explained in James 2:21-23. The justification in James 2:21 is justification by God, NOT man. Justification is the imputation of righteousness by God. Man cannot impute righteousness. The statement that what Phinehas did was "counted unto him for righteousness" is the same language used by God to describe Abraham's faith that was counted to Abraham for righteousness. "Abraham believed God, and it was counted unto him for righteousness." Romans 4:3-5.

> Was not Abraham our father justified by works, when he had offered Isaac his son upon the altar? Seest thou how faith wrought with his works, and by works was faith made perfect? And the scripture was fulfilled which saith, Abraham believed God, and it was imputed unto him for righteousness: and he was called the Friend of God. Ye see then how that by works a man is justified, and not by faith only. James 2:21-24.

When God Justifies a believer, he imputes the righteousness of Jesus Christ to that man. The imputation of righteousness to Phinehas in Psalms 106 means the imputation of the righteousness of Jesus Christ. It is a spiritual imputation. Why? Because no man is righteous. "As it is written, There is none righteous, no, not one." Romans 3:10.

We are justified only by God, not man. We can only be justified by God's grace through faith in Jesus Christ. "Being justified freely by his grace through the redemption that is in Christ Jesus:" (Romans 3:24) The only righteousness man can have is the imputed righteousness of Christ. "Even the righteousness of God which is by faith of Jesus Christ unto all and upon all them that believe: for there is no difference:" (Romans 3:22) Notice is says the faith "of" Jesus Christ. It is Jesus Christ who supplies the faith unto salvation.

That means that the righteousness counted to Phinehas was a *de jure* righteousness, not a *de facto* righteousness. Phinehas was not in fact righteous. He did a work prepared by God for him to do, whereby God imputed righteousness to him as a legal spiritual imputation. But that did not make Phinehas, in fact, a righteous man by his own doing. It was all God's doing, and Phinehas reaped the spiritual blessing of being justified by God.

Indeed, Phinehas was counted as righteous for evermore, that is eternity. "And that was counted unto him for righteousness unto all generations for evermore." Psalms 106:30-31. That is not some temporal righteousness before men as proposed by some; that is a spiritual eternal righteousness from God. Notice that it "was" (past tense) accounted at a given time by someone (God) for all time. No man can, at a given point, account someone to be righteous for "all generations for evermore." Only God can do that.

Righteousness is imputed to the believer by God. It cannot be imputed to a believer by man. To teach that the justification spoken of in James 2:21 is ONLY justification before men and NOT justification by God is heresy. The justification in James 2:21 is justification by God (NOT man), where God (NOT man) imputes righteousness to Abraham by his faith that was manifested in his works.

As we saw in the previous chapter, for man to declare another man justified is an abomination to the Lord. "He that justifieth the wicked, and he that condemneth the just, even they both are abomination to the LORD." Proverbs 17:15. All men are born wicked. "For all have sinned, and come short of the glory of God. Romans 3:23. Indeed, "there is none righteous, no, not one." Romans 3:10. It is only God who can justify a man. "Being justified freely by his grace through the redemption that is in

Christ Jesus." Romans 3:24.

6 The Arminian Apostasy

The insistence by many that James is speaking about justification before men and not by God is a direct result of a failure to understand that faith is by revelation from God. The gospel is that faith is imparted to a person by God. Ephesians 2:8-10; John 1:13; Hebrews 12:2.

That is why "we walk by faith, not by sight." 2 Corinthians 5:7. This spiritual reality is not known to most. They do not understand the concept that true faith will bear the fruit of that faith by God's will and not by the will of man. The true gospel is God-centered. The false gospel is man-centered. Under the true gospel, all things pivot from the will of God. Whereas, under the false gospel, everything pivots from the free-will of man.

This man-centered free-will doctrine infected the Protestant churches through Jacobus Arminius (1560-1609 A.D.), who was ostensibly a Protestant but was, in reality, a secret agent of the Vatican. The free-will doctrine has gone from being a fringe apostasy in the middle-ages to today being considered the orthodox view of the gospel held by most supposed "Christian" churches. After Arminius' death (1609), his supporters, led by Simon Episcopius, issued a remonstrance in 1610. The remonstrance contained five articles summarizing their divergence from the fundamental aspects of accepted Christian orthodoxy. After issuing the remonstrance, Arminius' followers became known as "The Remonstrants." That doctrine became popularly known as Arminianism, so named after Jacobus Arminius. The Christian objection to the five points of Arminianism was pejoratively labeled Calvinism.

The five articles of the Arminian Remonstrance are: Article 1: God's election is conditioned on the free will choice of man; Article 2: Jesus atoned for the sins of everyone in the world, both saved and unsaved; Article 3: While man is depraved, God provides a special (prevenient) grace to all men that partially awakens them from their depravity so that they can make a free will choice whether to believe in Jesus; Article 4: Man can resist the grace of God; Article 5: God assists one who is saved in resisting the temptations of the devil, but a person can by the exercise of his free will reject God and lose his salvation.[21]

The five articles of the Arminian Remonstrance were the focus of the Synod of Dordtrecht (a/k/a Synod of Dordt) in the Netherlands. The synod responded to the remonstrance in 1619 with The Canons of Dordt, wherein the Dutch Reformed Church rejected the teachings of Arminius.[22]

The so-called five points of Calvinism were actually developed from the Canons of the Synod of Dordtrecht in response to the Arminian Remonstrants and not from John Calvin, who had been long dead before the Synod of Dordtrecht met. The Arminians had to find a way to get out from under the cloud of heresy after their theology was refuted by an official synod of the Dutch Reformed Church. The Arminians came up with the idea of creating a straw man in John Calvin. Rather than argue that the theological dispute was Arminianism vs. the Synod of Dordt (or more accurately Arminianism vs. Christianity), the Arminians re-labeled the conflict as Arminianism vs. Calvinism. Once the Arminians succeeded in re-labeling the dispute, Arminianism could gain the false appearance of being on firmer theological footing.

The false gospel of salvation by the free will of man separates the method of salvation (faith) from the source of that salvation (God). Under the true gospel of Jesus Christ, saving faith is not from man; it is a spiritual gift from God. The gift of faith is bestowed upon the believer according to the will and good pleasure of God. Salvation is totally by the grace of God, not the will of man. "But as many as received him, to them gave he power to become the sons of God, even to them that believe on his name: Which were born, not of blood, nor of the will of the flesh, nor of the will of man, but of God." (John 1:12-13)

Arminians are fond of citing the passage in Philippians 2:12 out of context. That passage says "work out your own salvation with fear and trembling." Philippians 2"12. But they always neglect to continued reading to the next verse, which explains who is doing the working. The next verse explains: "**For it is God which worketh in you both to will and to do of his good pleasure.**" Philippians 2:13. It is the power of God that changes a heart and makes a man willing to turn to Jesus Christ. "**Thy people shall be willing in the day of thy power.**" Psalms 110:3.

The critical difference between the true gospel and the free-will anti-gospel is the object of the glory for salvation. God is deserving of glory, and he will not share his glory with anyone or anything. See Luke 2:14; Isaiah 42:8. For a more in-depth analysis of the heresy of salvation by the free-will of man, read this author's book, *The Anti-Gospel: The Perversion of Christ's Grace Gospel.*

Satan, however, seeks to take God's glory from God. Isaiah 14:14. His anti-gospel attempts to do just that. Salvation is by the grace of God. Ephesians 2:8. God chose a particular group of people for salvation before the foundation of the world. Ephesians 1:4. To believe in Jesus Christ and thus be saved from the eternal punishment for sin, one must be born again. Romans 3:28. The crux of the issue is the source of faith. The anti-gospel of Satan contends that the source of that faith is man; that man has the free will to choose to believe in God. The gospel of Jesus Christ, however, unequivocally states that God is the source of the faith. John 1:13.

Judas betrayed Jesus as prophesied by God hundreds of years earlier. Jesus stated, while praying to God the Father: "While I was with them in the world, I kept them in thy name: those that thou gavest me I have kept, and none of them is lost, but the son of perdition; that the scripture might be fulfilled." (John 17:12)

God planned the betrayal of Jesus by Judas. In Psalms we read a prophecy written many centuries before the betrayal of Jesus by Judas: "Yea, mine own familiar friend, in whom I trusted, which did eat of my bread, hath lifted up his heel against me." (Psalms 41:9) Jesus, referring to the prophecy in Jeremiah, told the apostles: "I speak not of you all: I know whom I have chosen: but that the scripture may be fulfilled, He that eateth bread with me hath lifted up his heel against me." (John 13:18)

Jesus knew Judas would betray him: "For he knew who should betray him; therefore said he, Ye are not all clean." (John 13:11) Judas had no more a free-will in the matter than a pencil has a free will to write. Judas, like the pencil, was an instrument completely under God's control.

God did not leave our salvation to the chance that Judas might not betray Jesus. God is love. 1 John 4:8. It would be the very antithesis of love to leave our salvation to chance. God is not a gambler.

God preordained Judas to betray Jesus. Judas had no choice in the matter. God predicted what Judas would do hundreds of years before he did it and then predicted it to his apostles moments before it happened. Jesus then personally gave Judas orders to hurry up and betray him. Judas could not resist the will of God.

> Jesus answered, He it is, to whom I shall give a sop, when I have dipped it. And when he had dipped the sop, he gave it to Judas Iscariot, the son of Simon. And after the sop Satan entered into him. Then said Jesus unto him, That thou doest, do quickly. (John 13:26-27)

Not only did Judas not have a free-will to choose whether to betray Jesus, but every single act of Herod, Pontius Pilate, the Jews, and the Romans was preordained and orchestrated by the sovereign God of Heaven. "For of a truth against thy holy child Jesus, whom thou hast anointed, both Herod, and Pontius Pilate, with the Gentiles, and the people of Israel, were gathered together, For to do whatsoever thy hand and thy counsel determined before to be done." (Acts 4:27-28) In fact, God orders the steps of all men and controls their very tongue. "The preparations of the heart in man, and the answer of the tongue are from the Lord." Prov. 16:1.

7 Hell Awaits Those Having Faith Without Works

It is provably wrong that the justification that is spoken of in James refers to the justification before men and NOT by God. James states that the justification that he speaks of is about justification before God at judgment. "So speak ye, and so do, as they that shall be judged by the law of liberty." (James 2:12) James explains that he is speaking about salvation. "What doth it profit, my brethren, though a man say he hath faith, and have not works? can faith save him?" (James 2:14) Faith without works cannot save.

Indeed, Jesus says that very same thing as he describes the final judgment. "When the Son of man shall come in his glory, and all the holy angels with him, then shall he sit upon the throne of his glory:" (Matthew 25:31) There can be no argument about it. What Jesus is going to describe is what happens at the final judgment. What does Jesus describe as the basis for judging people? He looks at their works.

James Explains Faith Without Works

"What doth it profit, my brethren, though a man say he hath faith, and have not works? can faith save him? If a brother or sister be naked, and destitute of daily food, And one of you say unto them, Depart in peace, be ye warmed and filled; notwithstanding ye give them not those things which are needful to the body; what doth it profit? **Even so faith, if it hath not works, is dead, being alone.** Yea, a man may say, Thou hast faith, and I have works: shew me thy faith without thy works, and **I will shew thee my faith by my works.** Thou believest that there is one God; thou doest well: the devils also believe, and tremble. **But wilt thou know, O vain man, that faith without works is dead?**" (James 2:14-20)

Jesus Explains Faith Without Works

"Then shall he say also unto them on the left hand, **Depart from me, ye cursed, into everlasting fire, prepared for the devil and his angels: For I was an hungred, and ye gave me no meat: I was thirsty, and ye gave me no drink: I was a stranger, and ye took me not in: naked, and ye clothed me not: sick, and in prison, and ye visited me not.** Then shall they also answer him, saying, Lord, when saw we thee an hungred, or athirst, or a stranger, or naked, or sick, or in prison, and did not minister unto thee? Then shall he answer them, saying, Verily I say unto you, Inasmuch as ye did it not to one of the least of these, ye did it not to me. **And these shall go away into everlasting punishment: but the righteous into life eternal.**" (Matthew 25:41-46)

Notice the parallelism. James makes the point that faith without good works cannot save a person; Jesus reveals that judgment in hell awaits those who do not have good works. That damnation would include those who have faith without good works. In Matthew 7:21, Jesus explains that important doctrine of the gospel. **"Not every one that saith unto me, Lord, Lord, shall enter into the kingdom of heaven; but he that doeth the will of my Father which is in heaven."** Matthew 7:21. James succinctly reiterates what Jesus taught. "But be ye doers of the word, and not hearers only, deceiving your own selves." James 1:22. When James says that "faith without works is dead" (James 2:20), he means that damnation awaits those that have faith without good works.

Notice also that the failure to do good is a sin for which one will be punished. **"Therefore to him that knoweth to do good, and doeth it not, to him it is sin."** (James 4:17) **"All unrighteousness is sin."** (1 John 5:17) It is not a suggestion by God that we love one another, it is a command. See Matthew 22:35-40. Any time we do not show charity toward another, it is a sin that must be punished unless that punishment is already taken on our behalf by Jesus Christ on the cross.

Those that are saved by God's grace through faith in Jesus Christ are cleansed from **"all unrighteousness."** "If we confess our sins, he is faithful and just to forgive us our sins, and to **cleanse us from all unrighteousness**." 1 John 1:9. At the final judgment, God sees only the righteous acts of his elect. Their sins are washed clean by the blood of Jesus Christ. "Come now, and let us reason together, saith the LORD: though your sins be as scarlet, they shall be as white as snow; though they be red like crimson, they shall be as wool." Isaiah 1:18. God has promised to forget all the sins of his elect. **"And their sins and iniquities will I remember no more."** Hebrew 10:17. A saved person will sin, but his sins are forgiven. The saved will then walk according to the Spirit and only the saved are capable of doing any good works because the works are the works of Christ who works through them.

Notice that the sheep had the fruit of their faith. They had good works that were done by Christ through them. It is heresy to suggest that the good works spoken of by James only justify a man before other men and are not works that are the fruit of justifying faith. The gospel is clear on this.

> When the Son of man shall come in his glory, and all the holy angels with him, then shall he sit upon the throne of his glory: And before him shall be gathered all nations: and he shall separate them one from another, as a shepherd divideth his sheep from the goats: And he shall set the sheep on his right hand, but the goats on the left. Then shall the King say unto them on his right hand, **Come, ye blessed of my Father, inherit the kingdom prepared for you from the foundation of the world:** For I was an hungred, and ye gave me meat: I was thirsty, and ye gave me drink: I was a stranger, and ye took me in: Naked, and ye clothed me: I was sick, and ye visited me: I was in prison, and ye came unto me. Then shall the righteous answer him, saying, Lord, when saw we thee an hungred, and fed thee? or thirsty, and gave thee drink? When saw we thee a stranger, and took thee in? or naked, and clothed thee? Or when saw we thee sick, or in prison, and came unto thee? And the King shall answer and say unto them, **Verily I say unto you, Inasmuch as ye have done it unto one of the least of these my brethren, ye have done it unto me.** (Matthew 25:31-40)

In Matthew 25:46, it was those deemed righteous who went into "life eternal." "And these shall go away into everlasting punishment: but the righteous into life eternal." Matthew 25:46. Do not loose sight of the fact that they were deemed righteous not by their works but by the faith that produced those works. Keep in mind that those works were the works of Jesus Christ. Christ was judging their works, but the only way to be righteous is by the imputed righteousness of Jesus Christ. The good works authenticated the faith of the sheep.

Righteousness is imputed to all who believe in Jesus Christ. Romans 4:22-25. "Even the righteousness of God which is by faith of Jesus Christ unto all and upon all them that believe: for there is no difference. Romans 3:22. Indeed, good works do not earn salvation. They are the fruit of that salvation. We are justified by faith. "But to him that worketh not, but believeth on him that justifieth the ungodly, his faith is counted for righteousness." Romans 4:5.

8 The Faith of Abraham

The key concept that must be understood is that "Abraham believed God, and it was counted unto him for righteousness." Romans 4:3. God is telling us that the faith of Abraham is the type of faith that makes one righteous in God's eyes.

> **Even as Abraham believed God, and it was accounted to him for righteousness. Know ye therefore that they which are of faith, the same are the children of Abraham.** And the scripture, foreseeing that God would justify the heathen through faith, preached before the gospel unto Abraham, saying, In thee shall all nations be blessed. **So then they which be of faith are blessed with faithful Abraham.** (Galatians 3:6-9)

Let us examine Abraham and his faith and see if we can determine if his faith was from God or from Abraham himself. First, let's look at the character of Abraham. Many think that God must have chosen Abraham because there was something intrinsically good in Abraham. When, however, we look at Abraham's behavior, we find that he was not intrinsically good. That should be no surprise, since God states that "there is none righteous, no, not one ... there is none that doeth good, no, not one." Romans 3:10,12.

Abraham was an example of an unrighteous man of which the letter to the Romans speaks. When Abram (he was later renamed Abraham by God) came into Egypt, he told his wife Sarai (her name was later changed by God to Sarah) to lie to the Egyptians and tell them she was his sister because Abram was afraid that since Sarai was so beautiful, the Egyptians would kill him in order to have Sarai. Technically, Sarai was Abram's half-sister. See Genesis 20:12. But the deception was that Abram misled the Egyptians to believe that was his only relation to Sarai. The most troubling aspect of the deception is that Abram was ungallantly willing to allow the Egyptians to have their way with his wife, Sarai.

> And it came to pass, when he was come near to enter into Egypt, that he said unto Sarai his wife, Behold now, I know that thou art a fair woman to look upon: Therefore it shall come to pass, when the Egyptians shall see thee, that they shall say, This is his wife: and they will kill me, but they will save thee alive. Say, I pray thee, thou art my sister: that it may be well with me for thy sake; and my soul shall live because of thee. (Genesis 12:11-13)

Abraham then allowed Sarai to be taken to Pharaoh's house. Pharaoh intended to make Sarai his wife. God, however, had to intervene to prevent that from happening.

> And it came to pass, that, when Abram was come into Egypt, the Egyptians beheld the woman that she was very fair. The princes also of Pharaoh saw her, and commended her before Pharaoh: and the woman was taken into Pharaoh's house. And he entreated Abram well for her sake: and he had

sheep, and oxen, and he asses, and menservants, and maidservants, and she asses, and camels. And the LORD plagued Pharaoh and his house with great plagues because of Sarai Abram's wife. And Pharaoh called Abram, and said, What is this that thou hast done unto me? why didst thou not tell me that she was thy wife? Why saidst thou, She is my sister? so I might have taken her to me to wife: now therefore behold thy wife, take her, and go thy way. And Pharaoh commanded his men concerning him: and they sent him away, and his wife, and all that he had. (Genesis 12:14-20)

Abraham's dissembling got him kicked out of Egypt. Abraham did the exact same thing to King Abimelech when he journeyed to Gerar with Sarah. Genesis 20. The episode with Abimelech was after God had justified Abraham by his faith in Genesis 15:1-6. God intervened in a dream to King Abimelech to prevent the king from sinning with Sarah. The heathen King Abimelech recognized that Abraham had sinned by allowing the king to take Sarah. King Abimelech railed against Abraham: "thou hast brought on me and on my kingdom a great sin? thou hast done deeds unto me that ought not to be done." (Genesis 20:9)

Understand that Abraham had committed this sin after being eternally justified by God through the faith that God gave to Abraham in Genesis 15:6. God has promised to forget all the sins of his elect. "And their sins and iniquities will I remember no more." Hebrews 10:17. A saved person will sin, but his sins are forgiven by God.

Paul explains the condition of a saved Christian in Romans 7:18-25. A Christian's heart is changed and we are freed from the power of sin. We can now obey the law of God, but since we are in the flesh, we will sin because no good thing dwells in the flesh. But all sin has been forgiven and all good works are ordained by

God that we walk in them.

> **For I know that in me (that is, in my flesh,) dwelleth no good thing:** for to will is present with me; but how to perform that which is good I find not. For the good that I would I do not: but the evil which I would not, that I do. Now if I do that I would not, it is no more I that do it, but sin that dwelleth in me. I find then a law, that, when I would do good, evil is present with me. **For I delight in the law of God after the inward man: But I see another law in my members, warring against the law of my mind,** and bringing me into captivity to the law of sin which is in my members. O wretched man that I am! who shall deliver me from the body of this death? **I thank God through Jesus Christ our Lord. So then with the mind I myself serve the law of God; but with the flesh the law of sin.** (Romans 7:18-25)

Abraham's sin against King Abimelech illustrates the point that one who is saved will still sin. But Abraham, nonetheless, bore the fruit of his salvation when, years later, he obeyed God. James explains that Abraham's faith was alive with works. His faith was the basis for being imputed with righteousness, but that faith was genuine faith given to him by God that bore the fruit of God. Faith without works is not saving faith; it is dead faith.

> **But wilt thou know, O vain man, that faith without works is dead?** Was not Abraham our father justified by works, when he had offered Isaac his son upon the altar? Seest thou how faith wrought with his works, and by works was faith made perfect? **And the scripture was fulfilled which saith, Abraham believed God, and it was imputed unto him for righteousness:** and he was

> called the Friend of God. Ye see then how that by works a man is justified, and not by faith only. (James 2:20-24)

God turns the repentant sinner away from his sin and toward Jesus Christ in faith. God must seek us because we will not seek God. "There is none that understandeth, there is none that seeketh after God." (Romans 3:11) The omnipotent God must intervene to make us willing. **"Thy people shall be willing in the day of thy power."** Psalms 110.3. God must intercede because we are spiritually dead, and God must quicken us. **"And you hath he quickened, who were dead in trespasses and sins;"** (Ephesians 2:1) We must be spiritually born again. John 3:3. Paul explains that if you are God's elect, he will **"[m]ake you perfect in every good work to do his will, working in you that which is wellpleasing in his sight, through Jesus Christ;** to whom be glory for ever and ever. Amen." Hebrews 13:20-21. It is God who is performing the good works of the believer according to God's good pleasure. That is because the Holy Spirit is in the believer and makes him willing to do good works. **"For it is God which worketh in you both to will and to do of his good pleasure."** Philippians 2:12-13. Faith in Jesus Christ will bear the fruit of good works. "[F]aith without works is dead." James 2:20.

We can see from Abraham's two episodes that Abraham was unrighteous, ungallant, and unfaithful. God did not choose Abraham based upon his good character.

God promised Abram (God later changed his name to Abraham) that he would be the father of as many heirs as the innumerable stars in the sky. Abraham believed God, and that belief was counted for righteousness.

> After these things the word of the LORD came
> unto Abram in a vision, saying, Fear not, Abram:
> I am thy shield, and thy exceeding great reward.

> And Abram said, Lord GOD, what wilt thou give me, seeing I go childless, and the steward of my house is this Eliezer of Damascus? And Abram said, Behold, to me thou hast given no seed: and, lo, one born in my house is mine heir. And, behold, the word of the LORD came unto him, saying, This shall not be thine heir; but he that shall come forth out of thine own bowels shall be thine heir. And he brought him forth abroad, and said, Look now toward heaven, and tell the stars, if thou be able to number them: and he said unto him, So shall thy seed be. And he believed in the LORD; and he counted it to him for righteousness. (Genesis 15:1-6)

From where did Abraham's belief come? Did Abraham's faith in God flow from Abraham's inherent stout character? No. Abraham did not have a faithful character at all. Whatever faith Abraham possessed was supplied by God, who was the "author and finisher" of Abraham's faith. See Hebrews 12:12. We later find that Abraham in his flesh decided to help God to bring about the promised heirs. He and Sarai (Sarah) decided to produce heirs by having Abram (Abraham) go in unto Hagar, Sarai's (Sarah's) Egyptian maid. Hagar conceived a child, Ishmael, that Abram and Sarai thought would be Abraham's promised heir.

> Now Sarai Abram's wife bare him no children: and she had an handmaid, an Egyptian, whose name was Hagar. And Sarai said unto Abram, Behold now, the LORD hath restrained me from bearing: I pray thee, go in unto my maid; it may be that I may obtain children by her. And Abram hearkened to the voice of Sarai. And Sarai Abram's wife took Hagar her maid the Egyptian, after Abram had dwelt ten years in the land of Canaan, and gave her to her husband Abram to be his wife. And he went

in unto Hagar, and she conceived: and when she saw that she had conceived, her mistress was despised in her eyes. (Genesis 16:1-4)

Abram was 86 years old when Ishmael was born. (Genesis 16:16) Thirteen years later, when Abram was 99 years old, God appeared to Abram and changed his name to Abraham because God said that Abraham would be the father of many nations. He also told Abraham that Sarai (who would now be called Sarah) would conceive and bear his promised heir, and his heir would be named Isaac. What did Abraham do? He fell on his face and laughed. Why did he laugh? Because he was 99 years old (Genesis 17:1) and Sarah was 90 years old. Abraham thought that it was impossible for them to have any more children. He argued with God to instead make Ishmael his heir.

And God said unto Abraham, As for Sarai thy wife, thou shalt not call her name Sarai, but Sarah shall her name be. And I will bless her, and give thee a son also of her: yea, I will bless her, and she shall be a mother of nations; kings of people shall be of her. Then Abraham fell upon his face, and laughed, and said in his heart, Shall a child be born unto him that is an hundred years old? and shall Sarah, that is ninety years old, bear? And Abraham said unto God, O that Ishmael might live before thee! And God said, Sarah thy wife shall bear thee a son indeed; and thou shalt call his name Isaac: and I will establish my covenant with him for an everlasting covenant, and with his seed after him. (Genesis 17:15-19)

Abraham in his flesh argued with God to make Ishmael the promised heir. He even laughed at God's prophecy. Abraham then sojourned in the land of Gerar and deceived King Abimelech in the same way he deceived the Egyptian pharaoh, telling King

Abimelech that Sarah was only his sister. Genesis 20. God intervened and prevented King Abimelech from sinning. God did not reject Abraham after his sin against Abimelech. God's election of Abraham was sure.

> And I give unto them eternal life; and they shall never perish, neither shall any man pluck them out of my hand. My Father, which gave them me, is greater than all; and no man is able to pluck them out of my Father's hand. (John 10:28-29)

Abraham sinned after God had promised to make him the father of nations through Isaac. God kept his promise; Abraham and Sarah had Isaac after Abraham sinned against Abimelech.

Abraham's righteousness was not a righteousness that was imparted upon him; his righteousness was a legal righteousness that was imputed to him by God. Abraham was made righteous in God's eyes through the faith that God provided for him. Abraham's faith and resulting righteousness were by the grace of God from beginning to end. "And he believed in the LORD; and he counted it to him for righteousness." (Genesis 15:6)

It was after Abraham was imputed with righteousness by God through his faith that Abraham unrighteously and ungallantly deceived King Abimelech about Sarah. Abraham's unrighteous deception of King Abimelech proves that God did not make Abraham in fact righteous in his flesh; the righteousness of Abraham was a legal righteousness imputed to him by God. God counted Abraham's faith (which God provided) to him for righteousness. Genesis 15:6; Romans 4:3; Galatians 3:6; James 2:23. In that same way, all who have the faith of Abraham to believe in Jesus Christ are imputed with the righteousness of Christ. "So then they which be of faith are blessed with faithful Abraham." (Galatians 3:9)

The Lord is a God of miracles. Sarah conceived and bore Isaac, just as God promised. Abraham was 100 years old when Isaac was born. Genesis 21:5. Isaac was the miraculous child of God's promise, not Ishmael, who was only the child of Abraham's flesh. There was nothing inherently good in Abraham that caused God to elect him. Abraham was an unrighteous dissembler who thought God needed his help in fulfilling his prophecy. Abraham was faithful only because God gave him faith. He was righteous only because righteousness was imputed to him by God through the faith that God gave to him in Genesis 15:6.

The faith that Abraham had when he was elected by God in Genesis 15:1-6 was accounted for righteousness for all time. Abraham could not be unelected by anything he did. His procreation through Hagar of Ishmael and his dissembling to King Abimelech did not disannul God's eternal election of Isaac as the heir of the promise. The faith that Abraham had in Genesis 15:6 was supernatural faith that came from God. That is what God means when he says that Jesus is the "author and finisher of our faith." Hebrews 12:12. Abraham's fleshly efforts to interfere with God's plan did not disannul that plan. God elected Isaac as the heir, not Ishmael. God knew what Abraham would do. It was not a surprise to God. Despite Abraham's fleshly interference, the yet unborn Isaac (indeed, he had not yet even been conceived) remained God's elect. Abraham kept the faith given to him by God in Genesis 15:16. "Who against hope believed in hope, that he might become the father of many nations, according to that which was spoken, So shall thy seed be." Romans 4:18. Abraham kept his supernatural faith, which was proven when God tried Abraham by commanding him to sacrifice Isaac. Genesis 22:1-18.

> By faith Abraham, when he was tried, offered up Isaac: and he that had received the promises offered up his only begotten son, Of whom it was said, That in Isaac shall thy seed be called: Accounting that God was able to raise him up,

even from the dead; from whence also he received him in a figure. (Hebrews 11:17-19)

Abraham thought that God would raise Isaac from the dead. Why did he think that? Because he believed God's original prophecy that Isaac would be the promised heir through which many nations would be born. Abraham knew that prophecy could not be fulfilled unless God raised Isaac from the dead. Ultimately, God stopped Abraham from sacrificing Isaac by calling from heaven to "lay not thine hand upon the lad, neither do thou any thing unto him." Genesis 22:12.

God further stated: "And in thy seed shall all the nations of the earth be blessed; because thou hast obeyed my voice." (Genesis 22:18) Who is that blessed seed? He is Jesus Christ. "Now to Abraham and his seed were the promises made. He saith not, And to seeds, as of many; but as of one, And to thy seed, which is Christ." (Galatians 3:16)

Abraham believed the promises of God, and God counted his faith as righteousness. So too it is with those who have the faith of Abraham; they are the spiritual seed of Abraham. The church of God is the promised spiritual great nation. Those that believe in Christ are Abraham's seed and the innumerable children that God promised Abraham. "And if ye be Christ's, then are ye Abraham's seed, and heirs according to the promise." (Galatians 3:29)

The key passage is found in Genesis 17:9. It states: "And God said unto Abraham, Thou shalt keep my covenant therefore, thou, and thy seed after thee in their generations." A covenant is a mutual agreement. Each party has promised to do something. What many miss is that God has set forth both his promise and Abraham's promise. In Genesis 17:1 God tells Abraham "walk before me, and be thou perfect." Genesis 17:1. In return, God promises to "be a God unto thee, and thy seed after thee." Genesis

17:7. How could Abraham be perfect? God provided a way for Abraham to keep his end of the bargain to be perfect by imputing him with righteousness.

God supplied Abraham with faith. That faith was counted as perfect righteousness for Abraham. "Abraham believed God, and it was counted unto him for righteousness." (Romans 4:3) Abraham did not have the capacity to believe God (Ephesians 2:1), so God supplied the faith. The faith of Abraham was a gift from God. Ephesians 2:8. Jesus is the "author and finisher" of Abraham's faith and indeed the faith of all God's elect. *See* Hebrews 2:2.

God fulfilled the requirements of both sides of the covenant he made with Abraham. That is what God meant when he said in Genesis 17:9: "And God said unto Abraham, Thou shalt keep my covenant therefore, thou, and thy seed after thee in their generations." God ensured that Abraham would keep his end of the agreement and "be perfect" by supplying Abraham's faith that was accounted unto him for perfect righteousness. God stated that Abraham's seed after him would keep the covenant. God ensures the perfection of his seed by supplying the faith that is accounted unto them for righteousness. John 6:37, 65; 17:2.

Salvation is not based upon anything intrinsically good in Abraham or in any of God's elect, it is based upon the intrinsic goodness and grace of God. Faith in Jesus Christ is accounted for righteousness. That faith is a gift of God (Romans 4) according to his sovereign will (Ephesians 1-2) without regard to the lineage or merit of his chosen (John 1:12-13). The passage in Genesis 17:1-9 refers to an everlasting covenant. That everlasting covenant is the New Covenant of Christ, which is fulfilled in Christ. It is a spiritual covenant.

God made a conditional covenant with Israel that is referred to as the Mosaic covenant. The blessings were conditioned on the obedience of Israel. Israel violated that covenant, and therefore, the blessings did not flow to fleshly Israel.

> Now therefore, if ye will obey my voice indeed, and keep my covenant, then ye shall be a peculiar treasure unto me above all people: for all the earth is mine: And ye shall be unto me a kingdom of priests, and an holy nation. These are the words which thou shalt speak unto the children of Israel. And Moses came and called for the elders of the people, and laid before their faces all these words which the LORD commanded him. And all the people answered together, and said, All that the LORD hath spoken we will do. And Moses returned the words of the people unto the LORD. (Exodus 19:5-8)

Notice that "all the people answered together, and said, All that the LORD hath spoken we will do." Exodus 19:8. In this covenant, the Jews agreed to fulfill the requirements of the covenant by their own effort. Notice that God did not say that they "shalt keep my covenant" as he said to Abraham in Genesis 17:9. God promised that Abraham would keep the covenant. In Exodus 19:8, however, the Jews promised to keep the covenant. God is showing us in these two different covenants the difference between the futility of attempted salvation by the works of man and the solidity of salvation by the grace of God. No sooner did the Jews agree to obey God in Exodus 19:8 than they immediately fell into idolatry.

> Saying unto Aaron, Make us gods to go before us: for as for this Moses, which brought us out of the land of Egypt, we wot not what is become of him. And they made a calf in those days, and offered sacrifice unto the idol, and rejoiced in the works of

their own hands. Then God turned, and gave them up to worship the host of heaven; as it is written in the book of the prophets, O ye house of Israel, have ye offered to me slain beasts and sacrifices by the space of forty years in the wilderness? Yea, ye took up the tabernacle of Moloch, and the star of your god Remphan, figures which ye made to worship them: and I will carry you away beyond Babylon. (Acts 7:40-43)

The history of natural Israel is one of continual sin intermixed with periods of repentance until God finally finished with them according to his foreordained plan. There is a spiritual Israel, the church, to whom the blessings in the Abrahamic covenant flow. God's true Israel is and always was the church. The church contains the children of the promise. "Now we, brethren, as Isaac was, are the children of promise." (Galatians 4:28) The church is the Israel of God. "For in Christ Jesus neither circumcision availeth any thing, nor uncircumcision, but a new creature. And as many as walk according to this rule, peace be on them, and mercy, and upon the Israel of God." (Galatians 6:15-16) The church is the temple of God. "Know ye not that ye are the temple of God, and that the Spirit of God dwelleth in you?" (1 Corinthians 3:16) The church is God's holy nation inheriting the promises made by God in Exodus 19:5-8. "But ye are a chosen generation, a royal priesthood, an holy nation, a peculiar people; that ye should shew forth the praises of him who hath called you out of darkness into his marvellous light." (1 Peter 2:9)

Abraham was the father of Isaac, who was the father of Jacob; Jacob (also known as Israel) had 12 sons that were the progenitors of the 12 tribes of Israel. Abraham was also the father of Ishmael, but because Ishmael was the son of Abraham's bondwoman, the bondwoman and Ishmael were cast out. Genesis 21:10-14. Through Isaac, who was the son of Abraham's wife, Sarah, were to flow God's promises to Abraham. Genesis 21:12.

However, Isaac had two sons, Jacob and Esau. The promise given to Abraham flowed not to Esau, but to Jacob. In fact, God states in Romans 9:13: "As it is written, Jacob have I loved, but Esau have I hated." See also Malachi 1:1-3. God elected Jacob (Israel) as the person through whom his promises would flow.

In each of Abraham's generations, the blessing to Abraham flowed according to the election of God. No blessing was obtained that was sought through blood or effort. The blessing did not flow through the firstborn son of Abraham, Ishmael; God worked a miracle and had Sarah bear a child of Abraham, who was Isaac. It was Isaac's bloodline through which the promised seed, who is Christ, would be born. Genesis 17:19-21, 21:3; Hebrews 11:18; Galatians 4:28.

While the promised seed, who is Christ, came through the bloodline of Isaac, the beneficiaries of the promise are not the blood lineage of Isaac. The children of the flesh are not the elect of God; God's elect are the children of the promised Christ; they are spiritual children. Romans 9:6-8. "For ye are all the children of God by faith in Christ Jesus." (Galatians 3:26) The promises to Abraham were to be fulfilled on behalf of spiritual Israel, which is the church. That doctrine is authoritatively explained in this author's book, *Bloody Zion*.

In Christ there is neither Jew nor Gentile; we are all one by faith in Christ. He is not going to divide us once again into Jew and Gentile. His church is his body which cannot be divided. 1 Corinthians 1:13. For a kingdom divided against itself cannot stand. Mark 3:24. The seed of the promises to Abraham is Christ and those who have the faith of Christ, his church, not fleshly Israel.

> But before faith came, we were kept under the law, shut up unto the faith which should afterwards be revealed. Wherefore the law was our schoolmaster

to bring us unto Christ, that we might be justified by faith. But after that faith is come, we are no longer under a schoolmaster. For ye are all the children of God by faith in Christ Jesus. For as many of you as have been baptized into Christ have put on Christ. There is neither Jew nor Greek, there is neither bond nor free, there is neither male nor female: for ye are all one in Christ Jesus. And if ye be Christ's, then are ye Abraham's seed, and heirs according to the promise. Galatians 3:23-29.

God told Abraham: "Sarah thy wife shall bear thee a son indeed; and thou shalt call his name Isaac: and I will establish my covenant with him for an everlasting covenant, and with his seed after him." Genesis 17:19. God reveals the spiritual truth of Geneis 17:19 in Galatians 4:28, where Paul states: "Now we, brethren, as Isaac was, are the children of promise." As Isaac was Abraham's physical seed, so also Christians are the spiritual seed of Abraham, through whom the everlasting covenant flowed. Isaac's miraculous physical birth is an allegory for the miraculous spiritual birth of those who are of the faith of Abraham. Christians are miraculously born again by the grace of God through faith in Jesus Christ. John 3:3. "Even as Abraham believed God, and it was accounted to him for righteousness. Know ye therefore that they which are of faith, the same are the children of Abraham." Galatians 3:6-7. The physical seed of Abraham are not the objects of the promise, it is only the spiritual seed that is born by the Grace of God through faith in Jesus Christ. "That which is born of the flesh is flesh; and that which is born of the Spirit is spirit." John 3:6.

Paul reveals that the seed of Abraham referenced in the bible is not a reference to the flesh of Abraham; the biblical seed of Abraham are those who have the promised faith of Abraham. They are a unique people made up of both Jews and Gentiles.

Paul explains that point in Romans 9:6-8:

> Not as though the word of God hath taken none effect. For they are not all Israel, which are of Israel: Neither, because they are the seed of Abraham, are they all children: but, In Isaac shall thy seed be called. That is, **They which are the children of the flesh, these are not the children of God: but the children of the promise are counted for the seed.** Romans 9:6-8 (emphasis added).

Romans chapter 11 explains the election of God. God has broken off fleshly Jews from his kingdom and grafted in Gentiles, who are grafted in based entirely upon his sovereign choice. God grafts in branches and breaks off branches according to his sovereign election. The grafting in is through faith, which is provided by God. However, that does not mean that Jews are beyond salvation. It simply means that salvation is entirely by God's grace through faith in Jesus Christ. "God hath not cast away his people which he foreknew." Romans 11:2. God's election is regardless of whether someone is Jew or Gentile. A Jew who believes in Jesus as Christ becomes a new creation. He becomes a spiritual Jew, a Christian. "For in Christ Jesus neither circumcision availeth any thing, nor uncircumcision, but a new creature." Galatians 6:15.

In verse 18 of chapter 11 of Romans, Paul admonishes against boasting. No true Christian could ever boast in their salvation. Boasting is evidence that one is not saved. That is because salvation is completely an act of the grace of God. A true Christian has nothing to boast about, since salvation is totally of God. The only boasters are those who would feel they have something to brag about. That would be those who feel that they have done something to merit salvation. Certainly, those who think that their faith is founded on their own free will have something to boast about. The problem is they believe in a god who does not exist. They do not believe in the true Jesus of the bible, who is the author and finisher of true faith. They will be cut off, because of their unbelief in the true Jesus of the bible. The false faith in the false impotent Jesus is the kind of unbelief spoken of in verse 20.

> Boast not against the branches. But if thou boast, thou bearest not the root, but the root thee. Thou wilt say then, The branches were broken off, that I might be graffed in. Well; because of unbelief they were broken off, and thou standest by faith. Be not highminded, but fear: For if God spared not the natural branches, take heed lest he also spare not thee. Behold therefore the goodness and severity of God: on them which fell, severity; but toward thee, goodness, if thou continue in his goodness: otherwise thou also shalt be cut off. (Romans 11:18-22)

Notice that in verse 22 the focus is on the goodness and severity of God. Everything depends on the sovereign decision of God. Those who do not continue in the goodness of God will be cut off. That is a fact. Paul is not saying that continuing is something that is up to the person; it is God who determines the continuing. It is the goodness of God that is the focus; those who are saved have no choice but to continue in the goodness of God because it is God who decides whether the person continues in his goodness. The continuing is based upon the goodness of God. All who do not continue in his goodness "shalt be cut off." That is the severity of God.

The passage in Romans Chapter 11 addresses the grafting in and cutting off; the grafting and cutting is done by God, not man. God is the root, not man. There is not a single action done by the branches in those passages. Even belief comes from God.

9 The Free-Will Misinterpretation of John 3:16

The misunderstanding of the source of faith is the principal reason for the misinterpretation of chapter 2 of the book of James and many other Bible passages that address the fact that fruits accompany authentic faith. Most wrongly think that faith in Jesus Christ comes from the free-will of man. Thus, they argue that since faith comes from man's free-will, then it must mean that good works come from man's free-will. They conclude that to preach that God requires good works to perfect faith constitutes a false gospel of salvation by works because they think that those good works come from the free-will of man. Thus, they reject the notion that saving faith requires good works.

The deluded purveyors of the free-will gospel do not accept that Jesus is the source of the faith. They do not understand the simple message in the gospel that it is the faith "of" Jesus Christ that saves. Romans 3:22; Galatians 2:16. They do not accept that the fruit of that faith, good works, also come from Jesus. They do not accept that we are new creations who walk in the good works prepared ahead of time by Jesus. Ephesians 2:10. They have adopted a man-centered false gospel that taints their reading of Bible passages.

An example of this free-will misinterpretation of the gospel is the Arminian misconstruction of John 3:16. Many twist that verse to mean what it does not say. That error is born from the concept that faith in Jesus Christ comes from man's free-will rather than being a gift from God. John 3:16 states that "God so loved the world, that he gave his only begotten Son, that whosoever believeth in him should not perish, but have everlasting life." *Id.* Without dispute, the passage is talking about God's love for the world. That is a given. The Arminian free will advocates, however, subtly deceive their followers by misinterpreting the words "so loved" to mean "loved everyone in the world so much."[23]

The Arminians argue that God has a great love for the world and everyone it. Dr. Jack Graham, pastor of the megachurch Prestonwood Baptist Church, for example, states that John 3:16 means that God loves everyone. He stated: "I can stand up here and say to you: God loves you, every person."[24] Graham elaborated: "It [John 3:16] doesn't say that God so loved the elect or God so loved his chosen ones, or God so loved part of the world. But God so loved the world. And you know, we better be careful about adding [to] and subtracting from the Bible and playing little theological games with truth."[25] Graham continues with: "Why don't we just believe the Bible and take God's Word as it is? God loves every person. That's what the Bible teaches."[26]

The highly esteemed Bible scholar, Dr. D.A. Waite of *The Bible for Today, Inc.*, agrees with Graham. Waite states:

> "That WHOSOEVER BELIEVETH IN HIM should not perish, but have everlasting life" shows that the OFFER of God's great love is for ANYONE who believes in the Lord Jesus as Savior. "WHOSOEVER BELIEVETH" does not restrict God's offer of salvation to some LIMITED group, but to EVERYONE in this wide world![27]

(emphasis in original).

The context gives us a clue as to the meaning of "world." In John 3:1 Nicodemus, who approached Jesus at night, is introduced as "a man of the Pharisees" and "a ruler of the Jews." In verse 10, Jesus called Nicodemus "a master of Israel." Jesus' point in saying that God so loved "the world" was to tell Nicodemus that God's salvation plan is not limited to Jews. God's love extends beyond the Jews to "the world." Jesus does not mean he loves every single person in the world; he means his love is not limited to Jews only, but that his love is for all of his elect in the world without distinction to whether a person is a Jew or a Gentile.

John 3:14-15 is a parallel passage to John 3:16. Jesus draws a parallel between Moses lifting up the serpent in the wilderness to save the Jews from the bites of the fiery serpents and how God so loved the world, made up of both Jews and Gentiles, that he gave his only begotten Son by lifting him up on the cross "that whosoever believeth in him should not perish, but have eternal life." John 3:15.

It was God who sent the fiery serpents among the Jews to bite them in the wilderness. *See* Numbers 21:6. When the people went to Moses and asked him to pray to God for help from the serpents. Moses did so, and God instructed Moses to raise a fiery serpent on a pole "that every one that is bitten, when he looketh upon it, shall live." Numbers 21:8. It was God who drove the Jews to look upon the serpent on the pole by sending the fiery serpents to bite them, just as it is God who draws his elect in the world (both Jews and Gentiles) to look to Jesus in faith.

Furthermore, Arminians seem to skip over John 3:8, which clarifies that those whom God saves are born of the Holy Spirit, who is completely outside the control of man. Jesus compares the Holy Spirit to the wind; the wind can be heard, but no one can determine from where it comes or where it goes. In like manner, people can perceive the Holy Spirit's effects in the rebirth of the elect, but no one has control over the Holy Spirit. Those in the world whom God loves are saved through the Holy Spirit by the sovereign "list" (will) of God, not through man's mythical will. The Holy Spirit goes wherever he listeth (wills). "The wind bloweth where it **listeth**, and thou hearest the sound thereof, but canst not tell whence it cometh, and whither it goeth: so is every one that is born of the Spirit." (John 3:8)

Notice that Jesus explains that the wind illustrates not only the work of the Holy Spirit in saving God's elect, but it illustrates the effect of that salvation. He explains that "every one that is born of the Spirit" is known by his effect, i.e., his good works. The wind both "cometh" to save and "goeth" after salvation to good works.

In the John 3:16 passage, the words "so loved" do not mean that God has a great love for everyone in the world, but rather that he has a particular kind of love for a particular people in the world. The context tells us what kind of love God has and for whom he had that love.

The word "world" has a different meaning in different passages. The context sometimes gives a clue as to what God means. For example, in Romans 11:12 the context clearly indicates that God uses "world" to refer to only the Gentiles. In John 13:1 God uses "world" to refer to the earth. In John 15:18-19 God used the word "world" to refer only to the unregenerate in the world, which does not include believers. In 1 John 2:15 God is referring to the material temptations. In 1 John 2:2 and 2 Corinthians 5:19 God refers to only those chosen for salvation out of the world. Those passages will be discussed in more detail in a later chapter.

What did God mean by "world" in John 3:16? To answer

that we must look at the context and the whole counsel of God found in the Bible. We read in John 3:3 that Jesus tells Nicodemus that he must be born again to see the kingdom of God. That is a spiritual rebirth that cannot be by the will of man or through the flesh. God made it clear just two chapters earlier that this new spiritual birth comes to those "[w]hich were born, not of blood, nor of the will of the flesh, nor of the will of man, but of God." (John 1:13)

Jesus was explaining the spiritual rebirth to Nicodemus when he said in John 3:16 that "God so loved the world, that he gave his only begotten Son, that whosoever believeth in him should not perish, but have everlasting life." "God so loved the world" in that context means that God loved the world in this way: "that he gave his only begotten Son, that whosoever believeth in him should not perish, but have everlasting life." The spiritual rebirth is all of God. God "so loved the world" with a special love whereby that he gave his only begotten Son for the salvation of his elect. His elect are then born again of the Spirit unto salvation. God's love is a special sacrificing love for his elect; it is not a general love for all.

Jesus' statement that he "so loved the world" in John 3:16 was made on the heels of his statement in John 3:14-15 that "as Moses lifted up the serpent in the wilderness, even so must the Son of man be lifted up: That whosoever believeth in him should not perish, but have eternal life." The point was that God "so loved the world" in the same way he sent the serpents among the Jews in the wilderness so that they would look to the brass serpent on the pole held by Moses. Only the Jews who were bitten looked to the brass serpent held by Moses to be saved from death by the snake bites. In that same way, it is only those whom God draws to Jesus who believe in him and are then saved from their sins. God "so loved the world" that he draws his elect to Jesus the same way he used the fiery serpents to bite the Jews thus driving them to look to the serpent held up by Moses. It was only the Jews who had been bitten by the fiery serpents who had any motivation to look to the brass serpent held by Moses; in the same way it is only those drawn by God who have any motivation to believe in Jesus. "No man can come to me, except the Father which hath sent me draw him: and I will raise him up at the last day." John 6:44.

God draws his elect to Jesus through hardship and infirmities. That is how God works. He makes his elect weak in the things of the world so that they can become strong in the things of the Spirit. Jesus explained that point to Paul when he told him: "My grace is sufficient for thee: for my strength is made perfect in weakness." (2 Corinthians 12:9) God may take that which is important in this world away from his elect to draw them to him.

Just as the Jews looked to the brass image of the serpent on the pole to be saved from death brought about by the serpents' bites in Numbers 21:6-9, so also God's elect look to Christ crucified, who was made sin on their behalf to take the punishment of their sin on himself, thus saving them from eternal punishment. "For he hath made him to be sin for us, who knew no sin; that we might be made the righteousness of God in him." (2 Corinthians 5:21) As explained in John 3:14-16, the Jews were saved from physical death by looking to the brass serpent, so also God's elect throughout the whole world (both Jews and Gentiles) are saved from spiritual death by looking to Jesus Christ.

Jesus was explaining _not_ that he loved the whole world and everyone in it, but rather that he loved the world in a particular way. To interpret John 3:16 to mean that Jesus loves everyone in the world makes God speak with a forked tongue. For in John 17:9 we read that Jesus would not pray for the world, but rather only those that his Father had given to him. "I pray for them: **I pray not for the world**, but for them which thou hast given me; for they are thine." (John 17:9) Clearly, Jesus does not love everyone in the world, for he would not even pray for them; he only prayed for his elect. God states clearly in Romans 9:13: "As it is written, Jacob have I loved, but Esau have I hated." Clearly, God does not love everyone in the world.

The Arminians argue that "whosoever believeth in him" in John 3:16 means that man has a free will choice to believe or not in Jesus. The Arminians seem to rewrite John 3:16 to say that whosoever "of their own free will" believes in Jesus shall be saved. John 3:16 says no such thing. John 3:16 is a statement of fact, not a statement defining the source of faith. It is a fact that whosoever believes in Jesus will have everlasting life, and that is what Jesus intended to convey in that passage. Salvation is entirely God's decision, God's choice, God's work, according to his sovereign mercy; salvation is by faith, which God supplies; it is not a free-will choice of man. "So then it is not of him that willeth, nor of him that runneth, but of God that sheweth mercy." Romans 9:16.

In John 3:17 Jesus makes clear that "God sent not his Son into the **world** to condemn the **world**; but that the **world** through him might be saved." It is obvious that in light of the entire gospel, the "world" referred to in John 3:17 could not mean everyone in the world, since we know that most will not be saved. *See* Matthew 7:13. God sent his son that the world might be saved. He did not send his son on a futile mission. God sent his son to accomplish salvation for the world. By "world" in John 3:17, God meant those whom Jesus saved. If Jesus is referring only to the saved world and not to everyone in the world in John 3:17, he must also have meant only the saved world in John 3:16.

John makes it even more evident in John 3:18 that the "world" is not everyone in the world, because Jesus states that "[h]e that believeth on him is not condemned: but he that believeth not is condemned already." There are those in the world who would believe on Jesus and those who would not, and it is only to those who would believe on him that he loves. Jesus saves his elect from condemnation; he does not save anyone else. Matthew

25:31-46.

God does not love those who are under condemnation, whom he has the ability to save and yet does not save. The true God of the Bible saves those he has elected for salvation and he condemns those he has elected for condemnation. *See* Romans 9. Those who are saved are chosen for salvation according to the election of God, not man. 1 Peter 1:2. That is what Jesus meant when he said: "Ye have not chosen me, but I have chosen you, and ordained you, that ye should go and bring forth fruit, and that your fruit should remain" John 15:16.

The mythical Arminian god, on the other hand, is powerless to overcome the free will of man and therefore leaves man's salvation up to his fleshly free will. There is no spiritual rebirth from God under the Arminian theology; it is left to man's mythical ability by his own free will to believe in Jesus. The Arminian god loves everyone but is a helpless spectator to the free will decision of man.

Arminians would object to that characterization of their theology and argue that they believe that God is omnipotent, and he knows the choices that individuals will make, but he still gives individuals the power to ultimately choose (or reject) salvation.

That leaves the Arminians with a theological problem. In John 3:17 Jesus states: "For God sent not his Son into the world to condemn the world; but that the world through him might be saved." The Arminian god cannot be omnipotent if John 3:17 is to make any sense. That is because the Arminian's believe that "the world" in John 3 includes everyone in the world, and their god sent his son into the world to save everyone in the world. Yet, the Arminians acknowledge that most people in the world are not saved. *See* Matthew 7:13. An omnipotent God would accomplish his goal of saving all those whom he has decided to save. The Arminian god cannot be omnipotent since he has failed to save everyone in the world. According to the Arminian theology, their god is foiled by the superior power of man's free will.

If one accepts the Arminians' argument that their god is omnipotent, that creates an untenable theological result. Arminians interpret John 3:16 to mean that their god loves everyone in the world, yet most of the world ends up in an eternal lake of fire. If, as claimed, the Arminian god were truly omnipotent, he could save those whom he loves and prevent their eternal destruction. Yet the supposed omnipotent Arminian god does not lift a finger to save his loved ones, and instead stands idly by while they ignorantly reject his love and are cast into an eternal lake of fire, where there is weeping and gnashing of teeth. Who casts them into the lake of fire? Revelations tells us that it is God Almighty, Jesus Christ, at the white throne judgment. Revelation 20:11-15.

So, the Arminian god is omnipotent and can save his loved ones, but does not do so and instead casts them into an eternal lake of fire. The Arminian omnipotent god has a perverse way to show his love. According to the Arminians, hell is populated with people whom their god loves. Whereas the true God of the Bible casts into hell those whom he never loved.

Since <u>not</u> everyone is saved, the truly omnipotent God must have decided to save some and not others. That is precisely what God states he has done in Romans 9. Therefore, God could not have meant everyone in the world when he states that "the world through him might be saved" in John 3.

God has redeemed only his people. "Blessed be the Lord God of Israel; for he hath visited and redeemed **his people**." Luke 1:68 (emphasis added). Jesus is the good shepherd. He did not give his life for the goats, but he gave his life only for the sheep. "I am the good shepherd: the good shepherd giveth his life for the sheep." John 10:11. The sheep are known in particular by God, and his sheep know him. "I am the good shepherd, and **know my**

sheep, and am known of mine." John 10:14 (emphasis added). Jesus did not come to save all people from their sins, he came only to save "his people" from their sins. "And she shall bring forth a son, and thou shalt call his name JESUS: for he shall save **his people** from their sins." Matthew 1:21 (emphasis added).

According to the Arminian mythology, God loves everyone in the world. But they theorize that most rebel and refuse his free offer of salvation, thus forfeiting (of their free-will) the gift of salvation. The Arminians have a difficult case, however, when it comes to Judas, who betrayed Jesus. We have already seen how the free will doctrine is contradicted by the prophesied betrayal of Jesus by Judas. Either Judas was preordained to betray Jesus by God or he had a free will choice to betray Jesus. There is no middle ground. Either one believes the gospel of Jesus or the Arminian mythology.

The case of Judas also poses a problem for the myth that God loves everyone. According to the Arminian free will theory, God loved Judas, but Judas of his own free will rebelled and betrayed Jesus. That Arminian interpretation of Judas' betrayal simply cannot be true.

In John 13:18 Jesus states in pertinent part: "I know whom I have chosen: but that the scripture may be fulfilled, He that eateth bread with me hath lifted up his heel against me." (John 13:18) Notice that Jesus explains that his betrayal is according to scripture prophecy. Where is the prophecy found? It is found in Psalms 41:9. That Psalm states: "Yea, mine own familiar friend, in whom I trusted, which did eat of my bread, hath lifted up his heel against me." (Psalms 41:9) Psalm 41:9 was written many centuries before Judas was born. So here we have God prophesying his betrayal at the hands of Judas many centuries before he was manifested in the flesh on earth.

Judas had no choice in the matter. He was preordained to

betray Jesus. God did not love Judas. Jesus called Judas a devil in John 6:70. "Jesus answered them, Have not I chosen you twelve, and one of you is a devil?" (John 6:70) Jesus pronounced woe against Judas and stated that it would have been better if he were not born. "The Son of man goeth as it is written of him: but woe unto that man by whom the Son of man is betrayed! it had been good for that man if he had not been born. Then Judas, which betrayed him, answered and said, Master, is it I? He said unto him, Thou hast said." (Matthew 26:24-25)

In John 17:12 Jesus called Judas the son of perdition. "While I was with them in the world, I kept them in thy name: those that thou gavest me I have kept, and none of them is lost, but the son of perdition; that the scripture might be fulfilled." (John 17:12) God did not love Judas. He never loved Judas. Judas was a vessel chosen for destruction, and God prophesied Judas' betrayal of Jesus many centuries before it happened. Judas was a vessel preordained and fitted for destruction. If Judas was preordained for destruction, as prophesied and fulfilled in the Bible, then the Arminian interpretation of John 3:16 that God loves everyone in the world cannot be true. God explains that some are preordained to be saved for glory, and others are fitted beforehand for destruction.

> Hath not the potter power over the clay, of the same lump to make one vessel unto honour, and another unto dishonour? *What* if God, willing to shew *his* wrath, and to make his power known, endured with much longsuffering the vessels of wrath fitted to destruction: And that he might make known the riches of his glory on the vessels of mercy, which he had afore prepared unto glory. (Romans 9:21-23)

Jesus is emphatic that he never loved those who will be cast into the lake of fire. "I never knew you: depart from me, ye that work iniquity." Matthew 7:23. God does not say he once loved them; he states clearly that he never knew them. Matthew 7:23 is a real problem for the Arminian claim that God loves everyone in the world, and yet people end up in hell because they exercise their mythical free will, turn their back on God's love, and choose of their free will not to believe in Jesus. If Jesus never knew them, how could he have ever held out any chance of salvation for them? The answer is ineluctable; God never held out a chance of salvation for them.

Those chosen for damnation were so chosen before the foundation of the world. God never knew them! *See* Matthew 7:23. "Then shall he say also unto them on the left hand, Depart from me, ye cursed, into everlasting fire, prepared for the devil and his angels." Matthew 25:41. Notice in Matthew 25:41 Jesus calls those who are cast into everlasting fire "cursed." God never loved them; they are cast into the lake of fire because they were cursed from the beginning.

The fact that God never loved the damned is confirmed by the fact that those chosen for salvation were chosen from the foundation of the world. "Then shall the King say unto them on his right hand, Come, ye blessed of my Father, inherit the kingdom prepared for you from the foundation of the world." Matthew 25:34. If those chosen for salvation were chosen from the foundation of the world, then the cursed ones cast into the lake of fire were also chosen for damnation from the foundation of the world. That means that God could not have loved everyone in the world as the Arminians claim is the case in John 3:16. When God states he never knew those damned to hell, he means, literally, he "never" "ever" knew them. The God of the Bible casts those whom he never knew into hell, he never loved them "ever." His word is clear on that.

When one reads John 3:16-18 in context, the gospel of grace is clear, and what Jesus meant by "world" is also clear.

Notice, that in verse 18 Jesus states "he that believeth not is condemned already." Jesus means that the condition of man is that he is already condemned. Man is unable to come to God, and so Jesus came to bring salvation to his elect.

Jesus explains that he was not sent into the world to condemn the world, but to save the world. The world he saved is the same world "God so loved." That world is the world made up of those who believe in him and are therefore "not condemned." John 3:18. The believers are "born again;" they are given a spiritual rebirth that is totally by the grace of God through faith in Jesus Christ. John 3:3.

> For God so loved the **world**, that he gave his only begotten Son, that whosoever believeth in him should not perish, but have everlasting life. For God sent not his Son into the **world** to condemn the **world**; but that the **world** through him might be saved. He that believeth on him is not condemned: but he that believeth not is condemned already, because he hath not believed in the name of the only begotten Son of God. (John 3:16-18)

Look closely at the four uses of the word "world" in John 3:16-18. First, "God so loved the **world**;" second, "God sent NOT his Son into the **world** to condemn the **world**;" third, he sen his sone into the **world** so "that the **world** through him might be saved."

Notice that the passage ends with God explaining the reason that Jesus was sent into the world: to save the world. God accomplished his goal. The point in John 3:16-18 is that God saved the world that he loved. Who are those that God saves? He tells us in verse 18 that those who believe in Jesus are saved. Those are the people in the "world" that God so loved and that he saved. Those are the people for whom Jesus died.

If, as claimed by the Arminians, the "world" includes everyone in the world, including those who are condemned, then God failed in his goal of giving his only begotten Son to save everyone in the world from condemnation.

We know that the Arminian view is wrong because God is omnipotent. If God wills that he is going to save someone, God will save that person. God's will is always done, both on earth and in heaven. *See* Matthew 6:10. "For with God nothing shall be impossible." Luke 1:37. God accomplishes all he sets out to do. "The LORD of hosts hath sworn, saying, Surely as I have thought, so shall it come to pass; and as I have purposed, so shall it stand." Isaiah 14:24. God can save all whom he decides to save. "In whom also we have obtained an inheritance, being predestinated according to the purpose of him who worketh all things after the counsel of his own will." Ephesians 1:11. God is an omnipotent ruler. "[T]he Lord God omnipotent reigneth." Revelation 19:6.

We know, therefore, that the "world" that God set out to save in John 3:16-18 was in fact saved. That "world" could only be those whom God elected for salvation by his grace through faith in Jesus Christ, and does not include (as claimed by the Arminians) those preordained to be condemned to hell.

Jesus made the point that God can accomplish what is impossible for man; he saves men from the penalty of their sins. When he was asked by his disciples who could be saved, Jesus stated: "With men this is impossible; but with God all things are possible." Matthew 19:26. Notice that Jesus states that salvation is impossible for men. The context of his statement is important. Jesus had just told his disciples that "[i]t is easier for a camel to go through the eye of a needle, than for a rich man to enter into the kingdom of God." Matthew 19:24. His disciples thought that salvation then was impossible and asked him: "Who then can be saved?" Matthew 19:25. Jesus made the point that salvation was impossible for man, but all things, including salvation, are possible for God. This impeaches the Arminian claim that man can choose salvation of his own free will. Jesus states that is impossible; only God can do the impossible of saving his elect.

The instance of the rich man in Matthew 19 completely eviscerates the Arminian position that Jesus died for everyone in the world and that all are given the ability to believe or not believe as they choose out of their own free will. Jesus is approached by a man who asks Jesus: "Good Master, what good thing shall I do, that I may have eternal life?" Matthew 19:16. Jesus tells him in pertinent part: "there is none good but one, that is, God." Matthew 19:17. Jesus is not denying that he (Jesus) is good, certainly Jesus is good, because he is God; Jesus is pointing out to the man that he (the man) is not good. So why is the man not good? Because the Bible tells us that all men are enslaved to sin and are evil. Romans 3:23-24; 7:14-25; Jeremiah 17:9.

What Jesus said next points out to all the futility of man to believe in Jesus without being spiritually reborn by God. Jesus tells the man to keep all of the commandments, and the man claims that he has done that. Jesus then tells him that he must do one last thing: "If thou wilt be perfect, go and sell that thou hast, and give to the poor, and thou shalt have treasure in heaven: and come and follow me." Matthew 19:21. "But when the young man heard that saying, he went away sorrowful: for he had great possessions." Matthew 19:22.

Jesus then explained to his disciples: "It is easier for a camel to go through the eye of a needle, than for a rich man to enter into the kingdom of God." Matthew 19:24. Jesus stated that what is impossible for man is possible for God. Jesus was making the point that it was impossible for the rich to give up his possessions and follow Jesus. To follow Jesus requires that a man be born again. Man cannot do that of their own will because their will is enslaved to sin. The man found it impossible to follow Jesus because he was enslaved to sin.

Most preachers, particularly Arminian preachers, opine that the man was not saved because he lacked faith. The passage, however, says no such thing. It simply states that he went away sorrowful because he had great possessions. When one looks to God's whole counsel, we see that the man was ultimately saved, which was manifested at some time after he spoke with Jesus. Going to the gospel of Mark we read: "Then Jesus beholding him loved him." Mark 10:21. If Jesus loved the rich man, then that means that the man was at some point saved. He may not have been born again with saving faith at the moment Jesus spoke with him, but it certainly came later. If Jesus loves someone, they will be saved. The gospel is clear that all those in the "world" "God so loved" in John 3:16 are saved; in John 3:16, "world" means only those that "God so loved."

The Arminian view, however, is that Jesus just let the rich man go his way into perdition even though Jesus loved him. The Arminians claim that God will not interfere with man's (supposed) free will. But let us look at what the Bible says about the love of God. In John 14:13, Jesus states: "Greater love hath no man than this, that a man lay down his life for his friends." Jesus then tells his disciples that they are not his servants, but rather his friends. John 14:14-15. Jesus then makes it clear: "Ye have not chosen me, but I have chosen you." John 14:13. Jesus laid down his life for his friends, whom he loved. All of those for whom Jesus laid down his life were chosen by Jesus; they did not choose him. That means that the "world" that "God so loved" in John 3:16 were saved by the sacrifice of the only begotten son of God, who laid down his life for his friends.

The modern Arminian model of evangelism bears no resemblance to how Jesus evangelized the rich man in Matthew 19. John Cheeseman explains why:

> I am convinced that much modern preaching which purports to be evangelical falls short of scriptural

teaching and has little in common with the example of the Master Evangelist, the Lord Jesus Christ Himself. How would much modern evangelistic preaching and writing answer the question of the rich young ruler, 'What must I do to inherit life?'? The following answer is probably typical: 'If I am to benefit from Christ's death I must take three simple steps, of which the first two are preliminary, and the third so final that it will make me a Christian: I must believe that I am, in God's sight, a sinner, that is, I must admit my need; I must believe that Christ died for me; I must come to him, and claim my personal share in what He did for everybody.' Under the third and final step is explained how the willing sinner must 'open the door of his heart to Christ', the Christ who waits patiently outside the door until we open it to Him.

It is undeniable that such an answer, or something like it, is frequently presented today, and those who use this method probably justify it by claiming that it includes the central doctrines of the gospel — repentance, faith, conversion, substitutionary atonement, the sinfulness of man, and so on. If someone 'takes the step' but later questions the validity of his conversion, he is assured, 'You took a simple step, you committed yourself to Jesus Christ, but then God performed a stupendous miracle. He gave you new life; you were born again.' The concluding advice is often given: 'Tell somebody today what you have done.' This answer bears little resemblance to Jesus' reply to the rich young ruler (Mark 10:17-22).

The following is a summary of some of the basic

doctrines or presuppositions of this modern gospel:

Unregenerate men can repent and believe.

Christ died for the sins of every man individually.

Committing oneself to Christ, or deciding for Him, or coming to Him, is an act which the sinner can do as he wills at any time; that is, it is an act of free will.

Although God may be said to have taken the initiative in a general sense by sending Christ to die to make salvation possible, in any particular conversion it is the sinner who takes the initiative by coming to Christ, and it is God who responds.

Now let us compare these doctrines with the teaching of scripture:

The unregenerate man cannot believe the gospel, because it is foolishness to him; spiritual truths are spiritually discerned, and he lacks the requisite faculty, being spiritually dead in trespasses and sins (1 Cor. 1:18; 2:14, Eph. 2:1).

It follows that he must be born again (which is the sovereign act of God) before he can repent and believe. Faith in Christ is the gift of God. Thus salvation is wholly of the Lord; He takes the initiative (John 3:3-8, Phil. 1:6, 29, Jon. 2:9, 1 Pet. 1:2).

There is no gospel command in Scripture to believe that Christ died for your sins. No one can have legitimate assurance of this until he has been saved and can make his 'calling and election sure' by wholehearted trust and obedience. Rather, the gospel command is to repent and believe in Christ as the only Saviour, believing his promises and casting oneself on His mercy. We have already seen that Christ died for the elect (or, for those who believe) (John 10:11—16; 15:13—14, Rom. 5:6—11, Eph. 5:25-27, Heb. 9:15).

This modern gospel is presented with no hint that God is sovereign and active in drawing to Himself those whom He has chosen. In Scripture these truths are not hidden lest they should cause offence; they are declared and even emphasized, since God is glorified when man can boast of nothing in himself as the cause of salvation. 'I contribute nothing to my salvation except the sin from which I need to be saved' (Acts 13:48, Matt. 11:25—30, John 6:63—65; 15:16, Rom. 9:14—24).

It is implied that Christ's death merely made salvation possible for all, the salvation becoming actual only on the condition of belief. But the Scriptures without exception speak of Christ's death as actually effective in itself, because of its substitutionary nature, to redeem, reconcile, ransom and save to the uttermost (Rom. 5:10, 2 Cor. 5:21, Eph. 2:13, 1 Thess. 5:9, 10, Heb. 10:10, 1 Pet. 1:18-20, 1 John 4:10, Rev. 1:5).[28]

The helplessness of man of his own unregenerate will to believe in Jesus without first being born again by the sovereign election of God is revealed by Jesus in John 10. Jesus states: **"I am the good shepherd: the good shepherd giveth his life for the sheep."** John 10:11. The Jews later approached Jesus at

Jerusalem and asked him if he is the Christ, to which Jesus states:

> I told you, and ye believed not: the works that I do in my Father's name, they bear witness of me. **But ye believe not, because ye are not of my sheep**, as I said unto you. My sheep hear my voice, and I know them, and they follow me: And I give unto them eternal life; and they shall never perish, neither shall any man pluck them out of my hand. My Father, which gave them me, is greater than all; and no man is able to pluck them out of my Father's hand. I and my Father are one.

Jesus is stating how he elects his sheep through faith. Notice that Jesus did not say they are not his sheep because they don't believe; he instead states that they don't believe because they are not his sheep. Such passages, found throughout the Bible, impeach the Arminian theology. Jesus is the good shepherd who gives his life for his sheep. Those who do not believe that he is the Christ are not his sheep. Jesus did not lay his life down for those who do not believe in him. In John 15:19, Jesus makes the point that he chose those who would believe in him "out of the world." Jesus' sheep do not choose him; Jesus chooses his sheep. John 14:13. The great love Jesus had of laying down his life for his friends is limited to only those who are his sheep, his chosen. Those passages put an end to the Arminian nonsense that John 3:16 means that Jesus died for everyone in the "world," both saved and unsaved.

God did the impossible of saving the "world," as he expressly stated he would in John 3:16-18. The "world" God saved is made up only of those whom God elected by his sovereign and omnipotent grace to believe in Jesus.

The single passage of the Bible that best sheds light on what is meant by John 3:16 is found in 1 John 4:9-10.

In this was manifested the love of God toward us, because that God sent his only begotten Son into the world, that we might live through him. Herein is love, not that we loved God, but that he loved us, and sent his Son to be the propitiation for our sins. (1 John 4:9-10)

In that passage, we see that John is pointing out that God manifested his love "for us" by sending Jesus "to be the propitiation for our sins." A propitiatory sacrifice is a sacrifice that appeases and satisfies God's need to punish sin justly. Obviously, Jesus was a propitiation only for the sins of those whom he chose for salvation.

If, as claimed by the Arminians, Jesus died for everyone in the world, God would be sending people to hell for sins for which Jesus already satisfied God. Under the Arminian view, where Jesus died for all of the sins of everyone in the world, the sacrifice of Jesus on the cross was largely ineffective. God was not satisfied by the sacrifice of the Arminian Jesus. Which means that the Arminian Jesus' sacrifice on the cross was not a propitiation. That simply cannot be! The propitiation by Jesus' sacrifice is the whole point of the gospel! The Arminian gospel is the different gospel that Paul warned us about. 2 Corinthians 11:4; Galatians 1:6.

Another point made in 1 John 4:9-10 is "Herein is love, not that we loved God, but that he loved us." It was God who loved us, and sent Jesus as a propitiation for our sins. Man is incapable of his own free will to love God. It was necessary for God to send Jesus to save his elect. Man's condition is that he does not love God, he sent Jesus not to condemn the world, the world was already condemned. God "so loved" the world that he sent Jesus to save the world, by sacrificing himself on the cross. The "world" God "so loved" was saved by the sacrifice of his only begotten Son who was a propitiation only for those he had chosen for salvation.

The God of the Bible has an unconditional love for his children; whereas the Arminian god has a conditional love for his children. The love of the Arminian god is conditioned on the free will faith of the Arminian believer. The Arminian god is a treacherous god, who the Arminians claim loves everyone in the world, but in the end, he casts most of his loved ones into a lake of fire to be tormented for all eternity.

The God of the Bible has an unconditional love for his children. God provides the faith for those whom he has chosen for salvation, because they are powerless in themselves to have faith. Jon Hendryx explains:

> God's love is unconditional for those He intends to adopt as His children. He does not make us meet a condition (faith) before He will love us, as the Arminian affirms. Rather, He meets the condition for us in Christ by doing for us what we are unable to do for ourselves, that is, giving us everything we need for salvation, including a new heart to believe. (Ezek 36:26).[29]

10 The Faith of Devils

Steven Anderson misinterprets 1 Corinthians 3:12-13. He claims that passage provides salvation to one who has dead faith. But that is not what the gospel says. Anderson contradicts the gospel thusly:

> What's he saying? He's saying, look someday our works are gonna be tested. I believe it's a reference to the judgment seat of Christ. And at the judgment seat of Christ our works are gonna be examined. And the works that had eternal value gold, silver, precious, stones, they will abide the fire and we will cash them in like a token for spiritual rewards and eternal rewards. [God will look at] all the things that we did that had no eternal value: your athletic achievements; your business achievements; all the things that you did artistically; things that just didn't have an eternal value. And they're not even necessarily bad things. I mean, he didn't say it was dumb; he said it was wood, hay, and stubble. Wood, hay and stubble are wonderful materials. They have their place. But they have no eternal value. So if you only lived your life doing things that have no eternal value, your works are gonna be

> burned up. ... This is people who make it into heaven by the skin of their teeth. ... They made it. They believed on Christ. ... **So, can you get to heaven without doing any good works worthy of any rewards? Absolutely!**[30]

For Anderson to suggest that faith without works can save a person indicates that he does not understand the gospel. James makes it clear that faith without works cannot save a person.

> What doth it profit, my brethren, though a man say he hath faith, and have not works? can faith save him? (James 2:14)

The answer to that rhetorical question is an emphatic, no! Faith without works cannot save a person. Such faith is dead faith; such faith is the faith of devils.

> Thou believest that there is one God; thou doest well: **the devils also believe**, and tremble. But wilt thou know, O vain man, that **faith without works is dead**? (James 2:19-20)

Another charlatan who thinks that one can be saved by dead faith that has no works is Dr. Bob Wilkin (ThM, PhD, Dallas Theological Seminary). Dr. Wilkin was a student of the late Zane Hodges, who was an apostate who thinks that dead faith can save. Wilkin's biography is posted on the Grace Evangelical Society website:

> Wilkin has served as an evangelist on the staff of Campus Crusade for Christ, a hospital chaplain, a pastor, and a college professor of Greek and Bible. He is the founder and Executive Director of Grace Evangelical Society (GES). ... Dr. Wilkin is the author of seven books (dealing with assurance,

eternal rewards, final judgment, inerrancy, Lordship Salvation, and tough texts) and hundreds of magazine and journal articles. He regularly speaks across the U.S. and overseas as well.[31]

The highfalutin Dr. Wilkin thinks that if one who has the faith of devils can be saved. Wilkin claims:

> For those unaware of the traditional interpretation of James 2, it basically says that "faith without works is dead" means faith without works is not faith. And the question, "Can faith save him?" is understood to mean that faith without works cannot eternally save anyone.
>
> That way of viewing the passage is seriously flawed. Faith cannot be non-faith. No matter what faith is lacking, it remains faith. And justification is by faith alone, apart from works (John 6:28-29; Rom 4:4-5; Gal 2:16; Eph 2:8-9).[32]

Let us read closely the passage that Wilkin cites in support of his heresy. Wilkin cites John 6:28-29:

> Then said they unto him, What shall we do, that we might work the works of God? Jesus answered and said unto them, This is the work of God, that ye believe on him whom he hath sent. (John 6:28-29)

That passage does not support Wilkin's argument. Wilkin seems to think that Jesus was taking about the works needed for men to do. But that is not what Jesus was saying. Wilkin fails to understand what Jesus meant. Jesus said: "This is the work of God, that ye believe on him whom he hath sent." Words have meaning. Jesus was pointing out it is the "work of God that ye believe." That means it is God's work that one believes in Jesus

Christ. Jesus Christ is "the author and finisher of our faith." Hebrews 12:2. Faith comes from God. True faith will have good works because "faith without works is dead." James 2:20. God has ordained that we be born again as new creations to walk in works he prepared for us to do. "For we are his workmanship, created in Christ Jesus unto good works, which God hath before ordained that we should walk in them." Ephesians 2:10. But the work is done by God. Saving faith is the work of God. And the works that are the fruit of that faith are the work of God.

Everything for our salvation is supplied by and through Christ. Our faith in Christ is the faith of Christ. See e.g., Romans 3:22; Galatians 3:22; Revelation 14:12. Notice that both James and Paul refer to saving faith as the faith "of" Jesus Christ. That indicates the Jesus Christ is the source "of" our faith.

> My brethren, have not the **faith of** our Lord Jesus Christ, the Lord of glory, with respect of persons. (James 2:1)
>
> Romans 3:22   Even the righteousness of God which is by **faith of** Jesus Christ unto all and upon all them that believe: for there is no difference.

Wilkin next cites to Romans 4:4-5. That passage also offers no support for Wilkin's position.

> Now to him that worketh is the reward not reckoned of grace, but of debt. But to him that worketh not, but believeth on him that justifieth the ungodly, his faith is counted for righteousness. (Romans 4:4-5)

Wilkin seems to think that Paul is speaking about all works of whatever kind. He is not. Paul is talking about works done to receive a reward. Paul is saying that works done to earn the reward of salvation are ineffective. Paul is saying nothing about the works that are the fruit of salvation.

Wilkin next cites to Galatians 2:16. Again, that passage does not support Wilkin's position.

> Knowing that a man is not justified by the works of the law, but by the faith of Jesus Christ, even we have believed in Jesus Christ, that we might be justified by the faith of Christ, and not by the works of the law: for by the works of the law shall no flesh be justified. (Galatians 2:16)

Paul is continuing his theme preached in Romans. A man cannot be justified by works. Justification comes only by faith in Jesus Christ. That passage is not addressing the topic addressed by James, who was addressing the genuineness of saving faith. Saving faith will bear the fruit of that faith. James was not claiming that the works merited salvation. Paul is addressing that issue. And Paul is emphatic in saying that works do not justify a person.

Finally, Wilkin cites Ephesians 2:8-9.

> For by grace are ye saved through faith; and that not of yourselves: it is the gift of God: Not of works, lest any man should boast. (Ephesians 2:8-9)

Notice how Wilkin, very slyly, left out the next verse in Ephesians at 2:10, which explains what is being said in Ephesians 2:8-9. That passage explains the relevance of works. While verses 8 and 9 explain that we are saved by grace through faith and not by works, verse 10 explains that we are spiritually reborn by Jesus Christ as new creations and ordained to do good works prepared by God for us to walk in them.

> **For we are his workmanship, created in Christ Jesus unto good works, which God hath before ordained that we should walk in them.** (Ephesians 2:10)

Why would Wilkin leave out Ephesians 2:10? He did not cite to it because that single passage impeaches his theology. His theology of salvation by dead faith is refuted by Ephesians 2:10, and so he simply left it out.

How does Wilkin address James 2:14? James says: "What doth it profit, my brethren, though a man say he hath faith, and have not works? can faith save him?" (James 2:14)

Wilkin claims the passage in James 2:14 is referring not to eternal salvation but rather temporal salvation. Wilkin states:

> Clearly born-again people do not need eternal salvation. They do, however, need temporal salvation from the deadly consequences of sin in their lives (cf. 1:15).[33]

Wilkin then explains how the Greek word, *sozo*, translated as "saved" in James 1:14, could be interpreted to mean temporal salvation from physical death or illness and not eternal salvation from spiritual death. Whenever someone resorts to textural criticism and segues into a discourse on what the original Greek word means, hang on to your hats, you are about to take a ride on the apostasy express. And Wilkin ends up at his final whistle stop: "In light of the other uses of *sozo* in James, one should at least be open to the possibility that temporal salvation is in view in Jas 2:14 as well."[34] Wilkin opines: "In my opinion even those who are five-point Calvinists should be open to the temporal salvation understanding."[35]

Wilkin cites to R. T. Kendall, who amazingly proclaims

that he "believes the person lacking temporal salvation in 2:14 ('Can faith save him') is the needy brother (of 2:6) illustrated in the next two verses (vv. 15-16). Thus his view is that faith without works cannot save the needy brother from his destitute condition."[36] That interpretation of James is, quite simply, absurd, in light of the context in which it is presented by James. But a desperate theology requires a desperate interpretation of scripture.

The passage that Wilkin will not touch is James 2:19 that states: "Thou believest that there is one God; thou doest well: the devils also believe, and tremble. But wilt thou know, O vain man, that faith without works is dead?" (James 2:19-20)

Wilkin explains: "I chose not to discuss Jas 2:19 and the faith of demons in the text of the article." He claims that others have already written on that verse; he then cites readers to articles written by others on James 2:19. He gives as his second reason for not discussing James 2:19 that "the argument that demons don't believe in monotheism and hence illustrate false faith is patently false."[37]

Wilkin is making a false strawman argument. James is not saying that devils do not believe in one God. He is saying that they do have such belief, but despite that belief, they are doomed to hell for eternity. James is saying that faith without works is as the faith of devils; such fruitless faith does not save.

Wilkin's says his final reason for not addressing James 2:19 is that "Jesus did not die for demons. There never has been, nor will there ever be, any eternal salvation for demons. Thus regardless of what they believe or do, they are ultimately doomed."[38] That is exactly the point being made by James. Just as the devils are doomed to hell and Jesus did not die for them, so also those who have faith without works are those who are doomed to hell because Jesus did not die for them. The fate of those who have faith without works is the same as the faith of the devils who also have faith without works. Such fruitless faith does not save.

Apparently, Wilkin has no good explanation for how his theology of faith without works is not the heresy of salvation by the faith of devils. And so, he "chose not to discuss Jas 2:19 and the faith of demons."

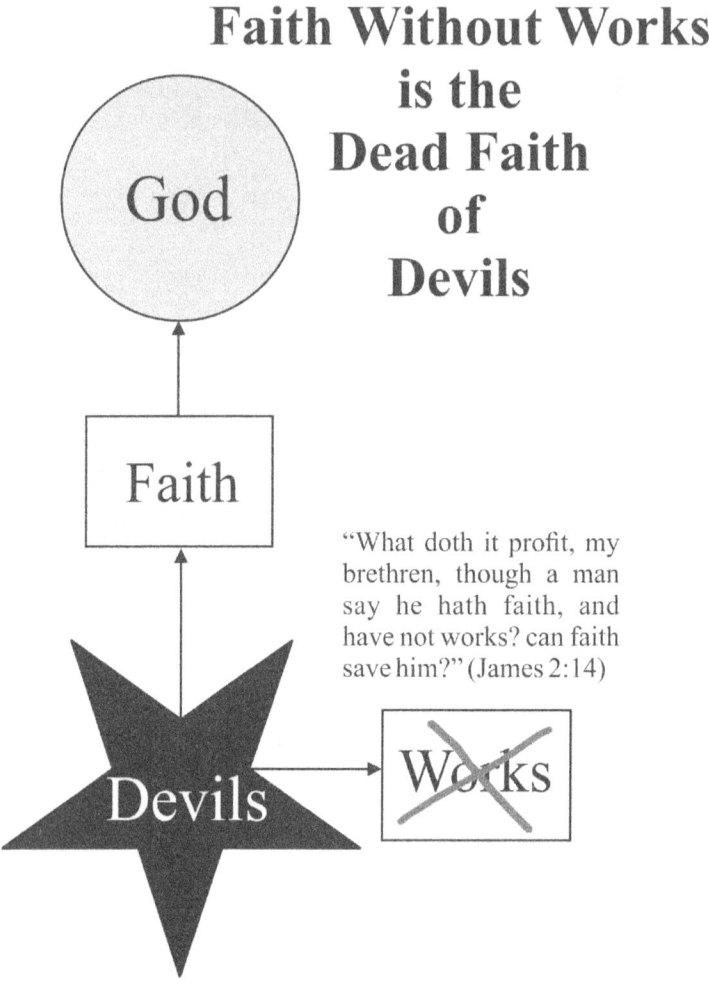

"Thou believest that there is one God; thou doest well: **the devils also believe,** and tremble. But wilt thou know, O vain man, that **faith without works is dead**?" (James 2:19-20)

11 Easy Believism

This faith of devils that does not save has been given a label. It is called "easy believism." Practitioners of easy believism view the gospel message as simply requiring intellectual faith. There is no spiritual regeneration; there are no fruits. Easy believism seems to be a euphemism because those who adhere to easy believism do not object to that label. Let's not use that euphemism. Let's call it what it really is. Peter calls it a damnable heresy; (2 Peter 2:1); James calls it dead faith that cannot save (James 2:14, 17) and the faith of devils (James 2:19).

Art Sadler examined the doctrines of one of the most popular purveyors of the dead faith gospel, Dr. Rick Warren, the founder and senior pastor of Saddleback Church in Lake Forest, California. That church is the sixth-largest megachurch in the United States, with a weekly attendance of more than 23.000 people. Warren is a best-selling author. He wrote *The Purpose Driven Life*, which alone has sold more than 30 million copies.

Sadler describes Warren's "Purpose Driven Church" movement that preaches the dead faith gospel to those on the wide road to destruction:

Fill the church with the unsaved, preach

easy-believism and watch the church grow. Easy-believism is the gospel without repentance and a change of life. You can gather a multitude around that type of a gospel. The multitudes of Christendom and the multitudes of the Cults verify that, but when you build a church on easy-believism, though you may have some Christians in it, you do not have the Church of Jesus Christ.[39]

This new gospel promoting dead faith removes Jesus Christ as central to the gospel. This new gospel becomes a man-centered gospel. The preaching is more of a class in psychology where Jesus Christ is an ornament. Sandler explains:

Rick Warren has stated, "It is my conviction that anybody can be won to Christ if you discover the key to his or her heart ... it may take some time to identify it but the most likely place to start is within the person's felt needs". This is psychology, not the gospel. The gospel does not consist of meeting the felt needs (desires), the sinner must turn from his or her own desires before they can be saved. This is another gospel, which is not the gospel. This is the ground work for easy-believism. Galatians 1:6, 7.[40]

Sandler explains that "Dr. Rick Warren, author of The Purpose Driven Life and The Purpose Driven Church has stated, 'When you reveal the vision to the Church, the old pillars are going to leave. But, let them leave, they only hold things up.'"[41] What does that mean to get rid of the old pillars? It means changing the doctrinal pillars of the gospel to create a new and different gospel. Warren eschews the fruit of salvation and preaches a dead faith. Sandler reveals some of the other doctrines that Warren has jettisoned to come up with his newfangled "purpose driven" gospel:

> The five fundamentals of the faith to which Warren objected are:
>
> - The inerrancy and full authority of the Bible.
> - The Virgin Birth and full Deity of Jesus Christ.
> - The bodily Resurrection of Jesus Christ from the dead.
> - Christ's Atoning, vicarious death for the sins of the world.
> - The literal Second Coming of Christ.[42]

Indeed, Jesus warned about men like Warren. Notice that the way to identify the false prophets, who are wolves in sheep's clothing, is by their fruit. Notice also how Jesus identifies those who have saving faith. Jesus explains that only those who both "heareth these sayings of mine, and **doeth them**" who are firm in their salvation and enter into the kingdom of heaven. The fate of those who "heareth these sayings of mine, and **doeth them not**" are those who were never known by Jesus and end up in hell.

> **Enter ye in at the strait gate: for wide is the gate, and broad is the way, that leadeth to destruction**, and many there be which go in thereat: Because strait is the gate, and narrow is the way, which leadeth unto life, and few there be that find it. **Beware of false prophets, which come to you in sheep's clothing, but inwardly they are ravening wolves. Ye shall know them by their fruits.** Do men gather grapes of thorns, or figs of thistles? Even so every good tree bringeth forth good fruit; but a corrupt tree bringeth forth evil fruit. A good tree cannot bring forth evil fruit, neither can a corrupt tree bring forth good fruit. Every tree that bringeth not forth good fruit is

hewn down, and cast into the fire. Wherefore by their fruits ye shall know them. **Not every one that saith unto me, Lord, Lord, shall enter into the kingdom of heaven; but he that doeth the will of my Father which is in heaven.** Many will say to me in that day, Lord, Lord, have we not prophesied in thy name? and in thy name have cast out devils? and in thy name done many wonderful works? And then will I profess unto them, I never knew you: depart from me, ye that work iniquity. **Therefore whosoever heareth these sayings of mine, and doeth them, I will liken him unto a wise man, which built his house upon a rock**: And the rain descended, and the floods came, and the winds blew, and beat upon that house; and it fell not: for it was founded upon a rock. **And every one that heareth these sayings of mine, and doeth them not, shall be likened unto a foolish man**, which built his house upon the sand: And the rain descended, and the floods came, and the winds blew, and beat upon that house; and it fell: and great was the fall of it. (Matthew 7:13-27)

The authentication of faith by good works is alluded to in the parable of the ten virgins. The wise virgins had oil for their lamps, but the foolish virgins had no oil for their lamps.

Then shall the kingdom of heaven be likened unto ten virgins, which took their lamps, and went forth to meet the bridegroom. And five of them were wise, and five were foolish. They that were **foolish took their lamps, and took no oil with them**: But **the wise took oil in their vessels with their lamps.** While the bridegroom tarried, they all slumbered and slept. And at midnight there was a cry made, Behold, the bridegroom cometh; go ye out to meet him. Then all those virgins arose, and trimmed their lamps. And the foolish said unto the wise, Give us of your oil; for our lamps are gone out. But the wise answered, saying, Not so; lest there be not enough for us and you: but go ye rather to them that sell, and buy for yourselves. And while they went to buy, the bridegroom came; and they that were ready went in with him to the marriage: and the door was shut. Afterward came also the other virgins, saying, Lord, Lord, open to us. But he answered and said, **Verily I say unto you, I know you not.** Watch therefore, for ye know neither the day nor the hour wherein the Son of man cometh. (Matthew 25:1-13)

Please carefully notice that it was not that the foolish virgins had oil but it was not enough oil. The foolish virgins "took NO oil with them." The distinction between the foolish virgins and the wise virgins was that the wise virgins had oil, but the foolish virgins had NO oil. Thus, those who have genuine faith will have good works and are like the wise virgins who had oil. But those who have faith without works are like the foolish virgins with no oil. There is no middle ground. One is either a saved sheep or a lost goat.

What is the oil spoken of by Jesus in that parable? In Psalms, the oil is a reference to God's anointing. The anointing is based upon the person loving righteousness and hating wickedness. "Thou **lovest righteousness, and hatest wickedness**: therefore God, thy **God, hath anointed thee with the oil of gladness** above thy fellows. All thy garments smell of myrrh, and aloes, and cassia, out of the ivory palaces, whereby they have made thee glad." (Psalms 45:7-8) A regenerated heart is in view in that passage.

Anointing with oil has always been associated with

holiness. "And thou shalt take the **anointing oil**, and anoint the tabernacle, and all that is therein, **and shalt hallow** it, and all the vessels thereof: and **it shall be holy**." (Exodus 40:9)

Anointing is a word often used to describe being imbued with the Holy Spirit. *See* Acts 10:38. Indeed, John elaborates using the symbolism of anointing, explaining that God has anointed us. That anointing leads us to do good works because **"every one that doeth righteousness is born of him."**

> But the anointing which ye have received of him abideth in you, and ye need not that any man teach you: but as **the same anointing teacheth you of all things**, and is truth, and is no lie, and even as it hath taught you, ye shall abide in him. And now, little children, abide in him; that, when he shall appear, we may have confidence, and not be ashamed before him at his coming. If ye know that he is righteous, ye know that **every one that doeth righteousness is born of him**. (1 John 2:27-29)

Notice the virgins had lamps. A lamp is a light to our walk. "Thy word is a lamp unto my feet, and a light unto my path." Psalms 119:105. John explains that "if we walk in the light, as he is in the light, we have fellowship one with another, and the blood of Jesus Christ his Son cleanseth us from all sin." 1 John 1:7. John's reference to walking in light is to walk in love. That is, our faith is manifested in good works of love for another.

Jesus calls the virgins with the oil in their lamps wise, whereas he calls the virgins with no oil foolish. All of the virgins had lamps, but only the virgins that had oil were allowed into the wedding feast. That is the same language he used in Matthew chapter 7 to describe those that were doers of his word and those who were not doers of his word.

Therefore whosoever heareth these sayings of mine, and **doeth them**, I will liken him unto a **wise man**, which built his house upon a rock: And the rain descended, and the floods came, and the winds blew, and beat upon that house; and it fell not: for it was founded upon a rock. And every one that heareth these sayings of mine, and **doeth them not**, shall be likened unto a **foolish man**, which built his house upon the sand: And the rain descended, and the floods came, and the winds blew, and beat upon that house; and it fell: and great was the fall of it. (Matthew 7:24-27)

The end for the foolish virgins in Matthew 25 is the same as the end for the foolish man in Matthew 7. He told the foolish virgins "[v]erily I say unto you, I know you not." Matthew 25:13. He told those who were like the foolish man, "I never knew you: depart from me, ye that work iniquity." Matthew 7:23. Their ends were the same. Jesus succinctly explains the lesson. "Not every one that saith unto me, Lord, Lord, shall enter into the kingdom of heaven; but he that doeth the will of my Father which is in heaven." (Matthew 7:21) It is the good works of Jesus Christ done through the believer that authenticates the faith of Jesus Christ imparted to the believer.

12   God Has Blinded Their Eyes

Dr. Wilkin and Dr. Warren are like so many other "Christian" theologians today who do not understand God's sovereign election. Among the reasons Wilkin gave for not discussing in his article James 2:19, wherein faith without works is identified as the faith of devils, was that there will never be any eternal salvation for devils. But that is true for those who have not been elected for salvation by God. Just as the devils were created to be sent to hell, so also the lost are created to be sent to hell.

In order to enter the kingdom of God, a man must be born again. John 3:3. It is not possible to birth oneself, God must do it. "**Of his own will begat he us with the word of truth**, that we should be a kind of firstfruits of his creatures." (James 1:18) Those who are born again have been chosen by God before the world was even created. "According as he hath **chosen us in him before the foundation of the world**, that we should be holy and without blame before him in love: Having **predestinated** us unto the adoption of children by Jesus Christ to himself, according to the good pleasure of his will." Ephesians 1:4-5.

Those chosen by God for salvation have done nothing to merit that salvation. We were not good; we were simply chosen, because God decided according to his own purpose to choose us. "Who hath saved us, and called us with an holy calling, **not according to our works, but according to his own purpose and grace**, which was given us in Christ Jesus before the world began." 2 Timothy 1:9. "In whom also we have obtained an inheritance, **being predestinated according to the purpose of him who worketh all things after the counsel of his own will**." (Ephesians 1:11) Jesus made clear to his disciples that they did not choose him, he chose them. "Ye have not chosen me, but I have chosen you, and ordained you, that ye should go and bring forth fruit, and that your fruit should remain: that whatsoever ye shall ask of the Father in my name, he may give it you." John 15:16.

God justifies a Christian. God does the choosing, not man. James 1:18. God does not love us because we first loved him. "We love him, because he first loved us." (1 John 4:19) It is an act of his Grace toward us that frees us from the bondage of sin. Once we are freed from the bondage of sin we can bear the fruit of righteousness. "But now being **made free from sin**, and become servants to God, ye have your fruit unto holiness, and the end everlasting life." (Romans 6:22) *See also,* Romans 5:16-19; 7:1-8:17. However, it is all a work of God, by his grace. **"For all have sinned, and come short of the glory of God; Being justified freely by his grace through the redemption that is in Christ Jesus."** (Romans 3:23-24)

Jesus states that his chosen are drawn by the Father to him. John 6:44. Those who do not believe in Jesus and are not saved do not believe because the Father has not drawn them to Jesus. "No man" can come to Jesus unless the Father gives him the faith to come to Jesus. In John 6:63-66, Jesus stated to those who "believed not" in him that they did not believe in him because the Father had not given them the faith to believe in him. The message of John 6 and the entire gospel is clear. Salvation is by the will of God and not by the will of man. *See* John 1:12-13. In John 6, many of the supposed disciples went back and walked no more with Jesus. They walked away from Jesus not because they were saved and lost their salvation, but as Jesus explained, because the faith to believe in him was not given to them by his Father.

> It is the spirit that quickeneth; the flesh profiteth nothing: the words that I speak unto you, *they* are spirit, and *they* are life. But there are some of you that believe not. For Jesus knew from the beginning who they were that believed not, and who should betray him. And he said, **Therefore said I unto you, that no man can come unto me, except it were given unto him of my Father.** From that time many of his disciples went back, and walked no more with him. (John 6:63-66)

The point is driven home in John 6 that salvation is by God's sovereign grace and that faith, which is the means of salvation, is a gift of God. In John 6:70-71, Jesus stated that one of the twelve he had "chosen" was a devil, referring to Judas. Judas did not lose his salvation; he was never saved to begin with, because he was not chosen for salvation. Jesus chose him for the purpose that Judas would betray him. Eleven were chosen for salvation and one (Judas) was chosen for damnation.

> **Jesus answered them, Have not I chosen you twelve, and one of you is a devil?** He spake of Judas Iscariot the son of Simon: for he it was that should betray him, being one of the twelve. (John 6:70-71)

Jesus lost none of those whom he had chosen for salvation. God preserves all who are chosen for salvation. Judas was preordained to be lost in order to fulfill the prophecy in scripture.

While I was with them in the world, I kept them in

> thy name: **those that thou gavest me I have kept, and none of them is lost**, but the son of perdition; that the scripture might be fulfilled. (John 17:12)

Judas was chosen for damnation before the foundation of the world according to the will of God, just as the other apostles were chosen for salvation before the foundation of the world according to the will of God. *See* Ephesians 1:4-5.

Jesus expressly told the Jews who confronted him in Jerusalem that they do not believe in him because they were not chosen to be of his flock.

> But ye believe not, because ye are not of my sheep, as I said unto you. My sheep hear my voice, and I know them, and they follow me: And I give unto them eternal life; and they shall never perish, neither shall any man pluck them out of my hand. (John 10:26-28)

Notice that Jesus did not say that if they were smart enough they could believe of their own free will. Instead, he put it right in their faces that they did not believe, and indeed they would never believe because they were not of his sheep. He said that to them after they asked him if he was the Christ. "Then came the Jews round about him, and said unto him, How long dost thou make us to doubt? If thou be the Christ, tell us plainly. Jesus answered them, I told you, and ye believed not: the works that I do in my Father's name, they bear witness of me." John 10:24-25.

Faith is not only the means of salvation, it is the fruit of the Spirit that is proof that God has elected the person for salvation. Man does not elect God by believing in Jesus, rather God elects man and gives him the faith to believe in Jesus. All who do not believe in Jesus were not elected by God for salvation. John Hendryx explains:

[W]e should take notice that Jesus tells us many times in Scripture why some do not believe. "You do not believe because you are not my sheep" (John 10). The order here is of great importance. Jesus does not say, "You are not my sheep because you do not believe," thereby making belief a condition of becoming a sheep. Rather, he says the exact opposite, "You do not believe because you are not my sheep." To believe therefore, far from being a condition, is the sign (or fruit) that one is already a sheep. So too, Jesus speaking to some of the Jews said, "Whoever is of God hears the words of God. The reason why you do not hear them is that you are not of God." The nature of the person determines the choice he makes. And who exactly is "of God"? Jesus answers clearly in his prayer to the Father in John 17:9 when he says, "I am praying for them. I am not praying for the world but for those whom you have given me, for they are yours." The Father has set apart certain persons for Himself and, in His prayer here, Jesus is seen to only pray for them, while simultaneously excluding others who were not "given" to Him.[43]

Chapter 6 of John makes clear that salvation is all of God. God "giveth" eternal life to his chosen through faith in his son, Jesus.

> Then Jesus said unto them, Verily, verily, I say unto you, Moses gave you not that bread from heaven; but my Father **giveth** you the true bread from heaven. For the bread of God is he which cometh down from heaven, and **giveth life** unto the world. Then said they unto him, Lord, evermore give us this bread. And Jesus said unto them, **I am the bread of life: he that cometh to me shall**

> **never hunger; and he that believeth on me shall never thirst.** (John 6:32-35)

Jesus makes the point in John 12:39-41 that God has blinded the eyes of the lost.

> Therefore **they could not believe**, because that Esaias said again, **He hath blinded their eyes, and hardened their heart; that they should not see with their eyes, nor understand with their heart, and be converted, and I should heal them.** These things said Esaias, when he saw his glory, and spake of him. (John 12:39-41)

God has purposely blinded the eyes and hardened the hearts of many to the gospel to prevent their conversion. Notice that Jesus stated that these things were prophesied by Isaiah. Clearly, God is not simply looking through the corridors of time and seeing whether men of their own free will would believe; God has determined beforehand who would believe and who would not believe. Isaiah 6:9-10, which was fulfilled in John 12:39-41, shows that God planned in advance that certain people would not believe in Jesus:

> And he said, Go, and tell this people, Hear ye indeed, but understand not; and see ye indeed, but perceive not. Make the heart of this people fat, and make their ears heavy, and shut their eyes; lest they see with their eyes, and hear with their ears, and understand with their heart, and convert, and be healed. Isaiah 6:9-10

In Romans 11:7-8 God makes the point, once again, that those who do not believe cannot believe because they were not elected to believe.

> What then? Israel hath not obtained that which he seeketh for; **but the election hath obtained it, and the rest were blinded.** (According as it is written, God hath given them the spirit of slumber, eyes that they should not see, and ears that they should not hear;) unto this day. Romans 11:7-8.

This is more than God merely omnisciently predicting who would not believe in him and thus be condemned; God is omnipotently determining who they would be ahead of time. God predestined those who would believe and those who would not believe; he "predestinated us unto the adoption of children by Jesus Christ." Ephesians 1:5. *See also* Ephesians 1:11; Romans 8:29-30. He chose those who would believe in Jesus before the foundation of the world. "According as he hath **chosen us in him before the foundation of the world**, that we should be holy and without blame before him in love." Ephesians 1:4. Concomitantly, God also chose those destined for destruction before the foundation of the world. Proverbs 16:1-4.

One cannot ignore the plain language in the Bible that God predestined his elect for salvation and also predestined the unelected for damnation. Many false preachers conjured an argument to get around those Bible passages. These free-will Arminians simply redefined the word "predestinate." Arminians claim that "predestinate" when referring to God's election of those to be saved is limited to mean only that God knows those who will exercise their free will and believe in Jesus. The Arminian interpretation is that "God in his divine foresight, looked down through the corridors of time and saw all of those who would choose salvation in Jesus Christ. Having this divine knowledge, He then ratified men's votes of confidence in His ability to save them."[44]

Romans 8:29-30 completely eviscerates the Arminian theology.

> For whom he did foreknow, he also did predestinate to be conformed to the image of his Son, that he might be the firstborn among many brethren. Moreover whom he did predestinate, them he also called: and whom he called, them he also justified: and whom he justified, them he also glorified. Romans 8:29-30.

John Wesley, a free-will Arminian and founder of the Methodist Church, tried to explain away the clear gospel of the sovereign grace of God. Wesley claimed that since God knows everything at any moment, he knows nothing ahead of time, and therefore he does not foreknow or predestinate anything. Wesley stated:

> The sum of all is this: the almighty, all-wise God sees and knows, from everlasting to everlasting, all that is, that was, and that is to come, through one eternal now. With him nothing is either past or future, but all things equally present. He has, therefore, if we speak according to the truth of things, **no foreknowledge, no afterknowledge.**[45]

The problem with Wesley's interpretation is that God himself in Romans 8:29-30 says that he does exactly what Wesley claimed God does not do. God makes it clear that he foreknows and predestinates his elect. Wesley is making up a different gospel out of whole cloth.

Wesley compounded his error by making the following incredible allegation:

> Yet when he speaks to us, knowing whereof we are made, knowing the scantiness of our understanding, he lets himself down to our

> capacity, and speaks of himself after the manner of men. Thus, in condescension to our weakness, he speaks of his own purpose, counsel, plan, foreknowledge. Not that God has any need of counsel, of purpose, or of planning his work beforehand. Far be it from us to impute these to the Most High; to measure him by ourselves! It is merely in compassion to us that he speaks thus of himself, as foreknowing the things in heaven or earth, and as predestinating or fore-ordaining them. But can we possibly imagine that these expressions are to be taken literally?"[46]

In essence, Wesley claims that God thinks we are too stupid to understand what he is really doing, and so he tells us a fib in Romans 8:29-30 about foreknowing and predestinating men. Wesley is calling God a liar. The brilliant John Wesley, however, was able to see through God's purported prevarication and understand the supposed truth that is the diametric opposite of the lies that Wesley alleges God tells in the Bible.

Wesley's free-will Arminian god is a liar who says he foreknows and predestinates, but actually does neither. The true God of the Bible, however, does not lie.

> God is not a man, that he should lie; neither the son of man, that he should repent: hath he said, and shall he not do it? or hath he spoken, and shall he not make it good?" (Numbers 23:19)

Wesley was a false teacher "who changed the truth into a lie." Romans 1:25. Despite Wesley's claims to the contrary, God is not lying to us when he says he foreknows and predestinates his elect. God means what he says. "Hath he spoken, and shall he not make it good?" Numbers 23:19.

John Wesley is just one of many wolves in sheep's clothing lurking about preaching a false gospel. Wesley admitted that he didn't even believe in the God of the Bible.

In a 1766 letter to his brother, Charles Wesley, John Wesley bared his soul and revealed to Charles his innermost thoughts. In that letter, which John Wesley never expected to be revealed publicly, he admitted that he preached a faith that he, himself, did not have. John Wesley felt "borne along" by some unknown force to do so. God would certainly not compel the preaching of a false gospel. It is, therefore, clear that the unknown force bearing John Wesley along to preach the Arminian gospel was the devil. That is an ineluctable conclusion from Wesley's own words:

> In one of my last [letters] I was saying that I do not feel the wrath of God abiding on me; nor can I believe it does. And yet (this is the mystery), **I do not love God. I never did. Therefore I never believed, in the Christian sense of the word. Therefore I am only an honest heathen**…And yet, to be so employed of God! And so hedged in that I can neither get forward nor backward! Surely there was never such an instance before, from the beginning of the world! If I ever have had that faith, it would not be so strange. **But I never had any other evidence of the eternal or invisible world than I have now; and that is none at all**, unless such as faintly shines from reason's glimmering ray. **I have no direct witness (I do not say, that I am a child of God, but) of anything invisible or eternal.**
>
> And yet I dare not preach otherwise than I do, either concerning faith, or love, or justification, or perfection. And yet I find rather an increase than a

decrease of zeal for the whole work of God and every part of it. I am borne along, I know not how, that I can't stand still. **I want all the world to come to what I do not know.**[47]

Wesley was 63 years old when he wrote that letter. The dirty secret of Wesley is that he was a heathen who did not believe in God. He preached a false gospel about a false god, in whom he did not really believe. How could Wesley so successfully preach a false gospel? Because people had been accustomed to ignoring God's words and accepting a contradictory gloss to those words.

Wesley's Arminianism was only a hair's breadth from atheism. There is little difference between the Arminian god, who minds his own business and leaves his creatures to their own devices, and no god at all. It is no wonder then that Wesley did not believe in God. His Arminian theology created a god in whom it is easy to lose belief. The devil, that subtle beast, could not have designed it any better.

13 The Malefactor on the Cross

Many cite the malefactor on the cross as an example of a person who had faith without works. They often argue that the thief did no good works. Even those who accept that James is saying that true faith will have works call the malefactor on the cross a "loophole" because "[y]ou must also realize he did not have an opportunity to do any works."[48]

It is true that the malefactor on the cross did not do any works to earn salvation. That is one lesson to learn. But there is another truth that many miss. We cannot conflate works to earn salvation with works that flow from salvation. The two are not the same. The malefactor did, in fact, bear the fruit of salvation.

> And one of the malefactors which were hanged railed on him, saying, If thou be Christ, save thyself and us. **But the other answering rebuked him, saying, Dost not thou fear God, seeing thou art in the same condemnation? And we indeed justly; for we receive the due reward of our deeds: but this man hath done nothing amiss. And he said unto Jesus, Lord, remember me when thou comest into thy kingdom.** And Jesus said unto him, Verily I say unto thee, To day shalt

> thou be with me in paradise. (Luke 23:39-43)

The malefactor on the cross bore the fruit of his salvation by rebuking the other malefactor and defending Jesus. He then turned to Jesus and called him "Lord." That is faith that God imparted into that thief. No person could have thought that a person being crucified next to him on a cross would be God. That takes a revelation from God for that thief to know that. It is the same revelation that is attendant to all God's elect who are saved by the grace of God through faith in Jesus Christ. All salvation is by the revelation of God. All faith comes from God. Saving faith will bear the fruit of salvation. In the end, the thief on the cross does not help the theology that one can be saved by a devil's faith with no works.

14 Running With the Devil

Dr. Joseph Dillow is another who believes that a person can have faith without works and nonetheless have saving faith. George Zeller of the Middletown Bible Church reveals that Dr. Dillow "received his Th.D. degree from Dallas Theological Seminary. He served on the staff of Campus Crusade for Christ, Christian Family Life, and as a visiting instructor in Systematic Theology at Trinity Evangelical Divinity School. For more than a decade, he and his wife Linda have lived in Vienna, Austria, where he has served as founder and director of Biblical Education by Extension International (BEE), a biblical training ministry for church leadership in eastern Europe, Russia, and China."[49]

George Zeller reveals that Dr. Dillow and Zane Hodges not only think that a person can be saved by the faith without works, but that same person can then proceed to live like a devil. Zeller examined Hodges' teachings and found that Hodges believes that a true believer can still be saved even though he abandons Christ and the faith. According to Hodges, a person could no longer believe in Christ and deny the facts of the gospel and still be saved. Zeller explains:

According to Dillow and Hodges, a truly saved

person can depart from the faith, abandon the faith, reject the gospel, mock Christianity, stop believing, and yet still be saved. Hodges believes that a regenerate person can totally defect from the faith (total apostasy) and completely withdraw his Christian profession, and yet still be saved.[50]

Hodges' heresy is a twist on the heresy of free-will Baptists who deny the preservation of the saints. Zeller explains:

> It is interesting to contrast Hodges' position with that of the Free Will Baptists. The Free Will Baptist position is that a true believer may depart from the faith and be lost forever. Hodges' position is that a true believer may depart from the faith and be saved forever.[51]

According to Zeller, "Hodges and Dillow insist that a saved person can bear no fruit, can persist in evil works (such as fornication, homosexuality, adultery, drunkenness, etc.) and yet still be saved."[52]

Hodges and Zillow's problem is that they seem to think that God has a hands-off approach to his elect. Nothing could be further from the truth. In Philippians 1:11, we read that a saved Christian is "filled with the fruits of righteousness, which are **by** Jesus Christ, unto the glory and praise of God." Thus, a Christian does good works because they are the "fruits of righteousness, which are **by** Jesus Christ." That is salvation comes with the fruits of righteousness that come from Jesus Christ.

If a tree brings forth evil fruit, it is an evil tree. A good tree will not bring forth evil fruit. Hodges and Dillow are just plain wrong to think that a good tree can bring forth evil fruit. They contradict Jesus Christ and say that a good tree can bring forth evil fruit.

Even so every good tree bringeth forth good fruit; but a corrupt tree bringeth forth evil fruit. A good tree cannot bring forth evil fruit, neither can a corrupt tree bring forth good fruit. Every tree that bringeth not forth good fruit is hewn down, and cast into the fire." (Matthew 7:17-19)

James explains the same concept with a different analogy:

Doth a fountain send forth at the same place sweet water and bitter? Can the fig tree, my brethren, bear olive berries? either a vine, figs? so can no fountain both yield salt water and fresh. (James 3:11-12)

Hodges gives an example of a friend of his who was a graduate of Bob Jones University and Dallas Theological Seminary. That man later proclaimed that he was no longer a Christian and often mocked and ridiculed Christianity.[53] The man bore evil fruit. But Hodges maintained that the man was nonetheless saved because he had once had faith in Jesus Christ. According to Hodges, the subsequent evil fruit was irrelevant to his salvation. Hodges' theology allows for faith without works to be considered saving faith.

That is the very behavior described by Peter. In 2 Peter, chapter 2, Peter warns against false teachers who shall bring in damnable heresies. Peter describes the dead faith heresy preached by Hodges, et al., to a T as a damnable heresy. Peter is referring to "chiefly them that walk after the flesh in the lust of uncleanness and **despise government.**" 2 Peter 2:10. What does it mean to despise government? That means to despise any limitation or control on their behavior. That is precisely what the dead faith purveyors like Hodges, et. al., preach. Hodges preaches that once a person has what Hodges calls "faith" (i.e., dead faith), he can live in sin without limit.

Peter states that these false teachers will promise liberty, but it is a false liberty. They are actually preaching enslavement to sin and corruption. These false teachers have learned the way of righteousness in the gospel. But they then eschew it and preach a fruitless faith whereby a man can go about sinning to his hearts content. Hodges is like a dog returning to its vomit.

> **While they promise them liberty, they themselves are the servants of corruption: for of whom a man is overcome, of the same is he brought in bondage.** For if after they have escaped the pollutions of the world through the knowledge of the Lord and Saviour Jesus Christ, they are again entangled therein, and overcome, the latter end is worse with them than the beginning. For it had been better for them not to have known the way of righteousness, than, after they have known it, to turn from the holy commandment delivered unto them. But it is happened unto them according to the true proverb, The dog is turned to his own vomit again; and the sow that was washed to her wallowing in the mire. (2 Peter 2:19-22)

John, as did James, explains that everyone who is in Christ is legally sinless. That means that in the sight of God, his elect have the perfect righteousness of Christ. Every act of a believer that is born of his faith is a righteous act in God's eyes because Jesus is doing it through them. That is what John means when he says that "[w]hosoever abideth in him sinneth not: whosoever sinneth hath not seen him, neither known him." Thus, when John says that "he that doeth righteousness is righteous, even as he is righteous" he is referring to the righteous works of Christ done through the believer. All who are not saved cannot do anything but sin. That is why John states that "[h]e that committeth sin is of the devil."

On the other hand, in the eyes of God, "[w]hosoever is born of God doth not commit sin; for his seed remaineth in him: and he cannot sin, because he is born of God." God does not see the sins of his elect because "his seed remaineth in him." John concludes with the truth that "[i]n this the children of God are manifest, and the children of the devil: whosoever doeth not righteousness is not of God, neither he that loveth not his brother." That message from John is the very message of James. Faith without works is dead. The works are those acts of love toward one another.

> Behold, what manner of love the Father hath bestowed upon us, that we should be called the sons of God: therefore the world knoweth us not, because it knew him not. Beloved, now are we the sons of God, and it doth not yet appear what we shall be: but we know that, when he shall appear, we shall be like him; for we shall see him as he is. And every man that hath this hope in him purifieth himself, even as he is pure. Whosoever committeth sin transgresseth also the law: for sin is the transgression of the law. **And ye know that he was manifested to take away our sins; and in him is no sin. Whosoever abideth in him sinneth not: whosoever sinneth hath not seen him, neither known him.** Little children, let no man deceive you: **he that doeth righteousness is righteous, even as he is righteous. He that committeth sin is of the devil;** for the devil sinneth from the beginning. For this purpose the Son of God was manifested, that he might destroy the works of the devil. **Whosoever is born of God doth not commit sin; for his seed remaineth in him: and he cannot sin, because he is born of God.** In this the children of God are manifest, and the children of the devil: **whosoever doeth not**

righteousness is not of God, neither he that loveth not his brother. For this is the message that ye heard from the beginning, that we should love one another. (1 John 3:1-11)

Hodges and Dillow are among those who hold the truth in unrighteousness.

> For the wrath of God is revealed from heaven against all ungodliness and unrighteousness of men, who hold the truth in unrighteousness. (Romans 1:18)

The admonition of Paul should be kept in mind. Those who bear not the fruit of the Spirit cannot be considered saved. Those who bear the fruit of the Spirit shall reap life everlasting. Their works do not merit salvation, their good works testify to that faith that brings life everlasting. Faith without good works is a dead faith that brings with it corruption.

> For he that soweth to his flesh shall of the flesh reap corruption; but **he that soweth to the Spirit shall of the Spirit reap life everlasting.** And let us not be weary in well doing: for in due season we shall reap, if we faint not. As we have therefore opportunity, let us do good unto all men, especially unto them who are of the household of faith. (Galatians 6:8-10)

Hodges and Dillow think that the dead faith of devils can save. And according to them, a devil's faith saves a person, who can then live a fruitless life and run with the devil right into heaven.

15 Loss of Rewards Heresy

Those that say that saving faith can have no works, find themselves in a quandary. They have a problem with what to do with good works. Since they have detached good works from salvation, they need to do something with them in order to give meaning to James. A separation of the works from faith itself necessarily results in the works being converted to merits, whereby the worker is owed a reward. Under this new theology, we are not saved by faith from God that has the fruits of good works from God, we are saved by faith (perhaps from God and perhaps not from God), and we add to that saving faith our own meritorious good works. The good works no longer perfect the faith; the good works, instead, perfect the person.

According to that corruption of the gospel, the reward is bestowed on the believer in heaven. And if the believer has not done enough good works, the believer will then suffer loss of rewards at the judgment seat of Christ. According to that theology, the believer will still get into heaven, but as Steven Anderson explains, they will "make it into heaven by the skin of their teeth."

There can be no compromise on the grace of the true gospel. Under the true gospel, God's grace flows to his elect. There is no merit that comes from man. Any watering down of the grace of the gospel is no longer the true gospel. Any amount of works that are accounted as merits establishes a false hybrid gospel of works. There can be no mixing of grace and works. **"And if by grace, then is it no more of works: otherwise grace is no more grace. But if it be of works, then is it no more grace: otherwise work is no more work."** (Romans 11:6)

Steven Anderson cites 1 Corinthians 3:12-15 to support the unbiblical view that one will lose blessings at the judgment seat of Christ. 1 Corinthians 3:12-15 states:

> Now if any man build upon this foundation gold, silver, precious stones, wood, hay, stubble; Every man's work shall be made manifest: for the day shall declare it, because it shall be revealed by fire; and the fire shall try every man's work of what sort it is. If any man's work abide which he hath built thereupon, he shall receive a reward. If any man's work shall be burned, he shall suffer loss: but he himself shall be saved; yet so as by fire. (1 Corinthians 3:12-15)

I Corinthians 3:12-15 is not addressing eternal rewards in heaven, it is addressing the testing of those in the church, whether they are truly saved as gold, silver, and precious stones or whether they will be shown to be lost as wood, hay, and stubble. That passage describes the church members being the material in the house of God and how well they will stand up to persecution and thus reveal their true character.

The heretical teaching of the loss of rewards doctrine is that, while a Christian will not lose his salvation, if a Christian sins or has insufficient good works, Christ will withhold rewards that would otherwise be given to him in heaven. Is that theory supported by scripture? No, it is not. The very theme of the Bible is that God's glorification of his elect in heaven is not a reward that is earned; it is a free gift. God's elect are sons of God who will be like Jesus in glory in heaven. 1 John 3:2. "We shall also reign with him." 2 Timothy 2:12. What reward possibly could be added to that?

If we are sons and heirs, what blessing will God hold back from us? All things will be bequeathed to us as gifts because God made us heirs. Titus 3:7; Romans 8:17. Our status as sons of God is the basis for our salvation. We are not rewarded for what God put in our hearts to do. God sees only the righteous works of Christ that he performed through us. All the good works done by Christians are done because Holy Spirit is in us performing the works that Jesus Christ ordained and prepared ahead of time for us to walk in them. Ephesians 2:10. Taking rewards away from Christians means that God is disinheriting his children. The loss of rewards theology has God going back on his word.

It is no surprise to find Anderson joined by John MacArthur in the loss of rewards camp. As you recall, they both interpret James, Chapter 2 as meaning that Christians are justified before men by their works. Anderson is an Arminian who believes in salvation by man's free-will, whereas MacArthur preaches sovereign election.

MacArthur believes that those whom God saves from their sins will nevertheless lose rewards for what they have done during their lives:

> The judgment seat of Christ then is this: a man goes who has lived believing in Jesus Christ, all of the works which he has done are there in the mind of God. It is then a process of God subtracting the worthless ones from the valuable ones and then rewarding the believer on the basis of the valuable ones that remain. The difference in rewards is only going to come because some believers have understood their priorities and they're going to

have a pile of valuable things while other believers, probably most, are going to have a monstrous pile of worthless things. . . . And you know this is the tragedy of so many Christians' lives that they don't live horribly immoral lives; they just live disastrously inconsequential ones. That really if they died there wouldn't be anybody in the world, spiritually speaking, who would miss them. And everybody's going to be saved, and everybody's going to have praise of God and there are crowns for all of us, but believe me there are some who are going to receive more than others. . . . There's the promise that awaits, either reward or loss. For some it's going to be a day of wonderful rewards. . . . But listen, beloved, I hesitate to say this, but yet I say it because it's in the word of God. **Some of you are going to be there and you're going to suffer loss.** You're not going to receive the full reward that you could have received. Why? Because you haven't lived the kind of life you should have lived. You haven't ordered your priorities. . . . **You can forfeit your crowns by some sin in your life.**[54]

MacArthur acknowledges that the loss is a result of sin. That is directly contrary to what the Bible states. The Bible states that Jesus died to take away all of our sins. John 1:29. MacArthur's theology sounds very much like a type of Purgatory. The Catholic mythology of Purgatory is based upon the fiction that if a person dies "in God's grace and friendship" but before he has done enough penance to atone for his own sins while living, he must go to a place called Purgatory, where he must "undergo purification, so to achieve the holiness necessary to enter the joy of heaven."[55] After an indeterminate sentence in Purgatory, where he is punished for his un-atoned sins, the person is then allowed entrance into heaven. The difference is that the mythical Purgatory is a temporary suffering as sins are purged, while most loss of rewards theologians have the Christian suffering shame, regret, and remorse for an eternity in heaven.

Where did Anderson and MacArthur get their unbiblical interpretation of 1 Corinthians 3:12-15? H.A. Ironside (1876-1951), was for 18 years the pastor of the Moody Memorial Church in Chicago and authored more than 60 books and pamphlets. He presents the popular misinterpretation of the passage at 1 Corinthians 3:12-15:

> But even though all one's work should be burned up, the Spirit of God tells us the believer himself shall be saved, yet so as by fire. But who that knows the saving grace of God and appreciates the love of Christ would wish thus to stand before Him? It is for Him we should labor. His glory should ever be before us, and then when we receive our rewards at His hand, it will be because of the delight which He Himself has found in our service.[56]

Lee Roberson, D.D., pastor of Highland Park Baptist Church for over 40 years, agrees with Ironside. In his book titled *Some Golden Daybreak,* Roberson interprets 1 Corinthians 3:12-15 to mean that Christians will stand before God at the judgment seat of Christ, with some Christians losing rewards and suffering shame for their works.

> If any man's work shall be burned, he shall suffer loss: but he himself shall be saved; yet so as by fire." You will remember that we said only saved people stand at this judgment; therefore, we cannot lose our souls, for we are standing there in resurrection and translated bodies. We will not lose Heaven at the judgment seat, but we can lose

our reward. ... Yes, we must stand before the judgment seat of Christ. Will you be happy, proud, and rejoicing as you look into the face of the Saviour, or will you bow your head in shame?[57]

James Melton takes Ironside's interpretation of 1 Corinthians 3:12-15 a step further. Melton claims that Christians will receive rewards based upon their personal good works. Melton claims that those saints without sufficient good works will receive "trash" from God.

> A fine companion passage for this is I Corinthians 3:11-15 ... Godly Christian service produces TREASURE in Heaven for the Christian. At the Judgment Seat of Christ, we (Christians) will receive our rewards. ... Most people are only concerned with going to Heaven or Hell, if even that, but the Bible instructs us to be concerned about our REWARDS. My eternal RESIDENCE was settled when I trusted Jesus Christ as my Saviour, but my eternal REWARDS are only settled when I deny myself and serve God in the Spirit. ... According to I Corinthians 3:11-15, the Judgment Seat of Christ will reveal gold, silver and precious stones for some Christians, but wood, hay, and stubble for others. Some will have treasures, while others will have trash. What will YOU have when you stand before your Lord?[58] (emphasis in original).

Dr. Douglas Stauffer takes 1 Corinthians 3:12-15 even further than Melton. He seems to accomplish the devil's desire, sending Christians to hell, for Stauffer presents a rather hellish version of heaven awaiting Christians. Stauffer states that "those that claim that Christians need only be concerned with a loss of rewards at the Judgment Seat of Christ never consider that the

Bible clearly points out that we will receive for the wrong too."[59] Stauffer claims that Christians will not just lose rewards in heaven for their unrighteousness, but will also be subjected to punishment, "shame," and even "condemnation."[60] Stauffer states that Christians will be punished for their sins in heaven: "Because of the preachers' understanding of the terror of the Lord, we should be warning Christians to live for God. God is not mocked. We are not 'getting away with our sin' down here."[61]

To suggest that somehow God will hold his elect to account for some failure to do good is wholly impeached by the scriptures. In Romans, chapter 8, we read that all those whom God foreknew he predestinated and called and justified and glorified. Romans 8:29-30. With what glory does he glorify his elect? God glorifies them by conforming them to the very image of his Son. Romans 8:29. If his elect are in the image of Jesus Christ, how can there be any loss of rewards? It is impossible. Indeed, immediately after Paul explains in Romans, chapter 8, that God's elect are chosen to be glorified, he asks the rhetorical questions:

> What shall we then say to these things? If God be for us, who can be against us? He that spared not his own Son, but delivered him up for us all, how shall he not with him also freely give us all things? Who shall lay any thing to the charge of God's elect? It is God that justifieth. Who is he that condemneth? It is Christ that died, yea rather, that is risen again, who is even at the right hand of God, who also maketh intercession for us. Romans 8:31-34.

Indeed, "who shall lay any thing to the charge of God's elect?" The answer is no one; for they will be conformed to the image of the Son of God, Jesus Christ himself, who is the "firstborn among many brethren." Romans 8:29.

1 Corinthians 3:12-15 does not support the proposition that the believer loses eternal blessings. If we read the passage in context we see that it addresses the building of the temple of God, which is made up of believers. The verse following the verse on works being burned up states: **"Know ye not that ye are the temple of God**, and that the Spirit of God dwelleth in you?" (1 Corinthians 3:16) The verses that lead into the description of gold, silver, precious stones, wood, hay stubble state: "According to the grace of God which is given unto me, as a wise masterbuilder, I have laid the foundation, and another buildeth thereon. But let every man take heed how he buildeth thereupon. For other foundation can no man lay than that is laid, which is Jesus Christ." (1 Corinthians 3:10-11)

The entire passage in 1 Corinthians 3 is a metaphor that addresses the building of the temple of believers - the church of Christ. The loss suffered in 1 Corinthians 3 is by the person who preaches the gospel to those who seemed to be saved but turn out to be pretenders, who flee the faith when exposed to the fires of persecution.

The fire of persecution reveals the resilience of the building material used to build the church. The gold, silver, and precious stones are Christians who will survive the fire of persecution, whereas the wood, hay, and stubble are nominal false-Christians who will be consumed by the fires of persecution and disappear from the church. The preacher suffers loss of the wood, hay, and stubble he brought into the church, but he does not lose his own salvation. The preacher himself is saved, and he will persevere during the fires of persecution.

In Hebrews 3, God states that Jesus is worthy of more glory than Moses, just as the builder of the house is worthy of more glory than the house itself. He is equating Jesus as the builder with the house, being Moses. God then states that Christ is the son over his house and that we Christians are his house, just as Moses is his house. The house, like the temple in 1 Corinthians 3, is an allegory for Christ's church of believers. Where Christ, who is the chief corner stone, is the builder of that house, made up of believers. We are one with Christ, his "holy brethren."

> Wherefore, **holy brethren**, partakers of the heavenly calling, consider the Apostle and High Priest of our profession, Christ Jesus; Who was faithful to him that appointed him, as also Moses was faithful in all his house. For this man was counted worthy of more glory than Moses, inasmuch as he **who hath builded the house hath more honour than the house**. For every house is builded by some man; but **he that built all things *is* God**. And Moses verily *was* faithful in all his house, as a servant, for a testimony of those things which were to be spoken after; But **Christ as a son over his own house; whose house are we**, if we hold fast the confidence and the rejoicing of the hope firm unto the end. (Hebrews 3:1-6)

1 Corinthians 3 states that the "day" declares the works of men and it is revealed by fire. What is the day to which God refers? It is a reference to the open revelation in this temporal world. Jesus explained in John 9: "I must work the works of him that sent me, **while it is day**: the night cometh, when no man can work." (John 9:4) Notice that Jesus was talking about working the works of God in present tense "while it is day." He meant right then and there on earth. The day to which he was referring was the opportunity to put faith, love, and hope into action then and there. He set the example for all Christians by being perfectly righteous while it was day. We are his "children of the day."

> But ye, brethren, are not in darkness, that that day should overtake you as a thief. Ye are all the children of light, and the **children of the day**: we

> are not of the night, nor of darkness. Therefore let us not sleep, as do others; but let us watch and be sober. For they that sleep sleep in the night; and they that be drunken are drunken in the night. But let us, who are **of the <u>day</u>**, be sober, putting on the breastplate of faith and love; and for an helmet, the hope of salvation." (1 Thessalonians 5:4-8)

What does 1 Corinthians 3:13 mean when it says that works will be revealed by fire? John the Baptist explained in Matthew 3:

> I indeed baptize you with water unto repentance: but he that cometh after me is mightier than I, whose shoes I am not worthy to bear: **he shall baptize you with the Holy Ghost, and with fire**: Whose fan *is* in his hand, **and he will throughly purge his floor, and gather his wheat into the garner; but he will burn up the chaff with unquenchable fire.** (Matthew 3:11-12)

John the Baptist stated that Jesus would baptize "with the Holy Ghost, and with fire." So the fire that is referred to in 1 Corinthians 3:13 must be a baptism of fire. What does that mean? 1 Peter 4:12-19 helps explain what this baptism of fire means.

> Beloved, think it not strange concerning **the fiery trial which is to try you**, as though some strange thing happened unto you: But rejoice, inasmuch as **ye are partakers of Christ's sufferings**; that, when his glory shall be revealed, ye may be glad also with exceeding joy. If ye be reproached for the name of Christ, happy are ye; for the spirit of glory and of God resteth upon you: on their part he is evil spoken of, but on your part he is glorified. But let none of you suffer as a murderer, or *as* a thief,

> or *as* an evildoer, or as a busybody in other men's matters. Yet if any man suffer as a Christian, let him not be ashamed; but let him glorify God on this behalf. **For the time is come that judgment must begin at the house of God: and if *it* first *begin* at us, what shall the end be of them that obey not the gospel of God?** And if the righteous scarcely be saved, where shall the ungodly and the sinner appear? Wherefore **let them that suffer according to the will of God commit the keeping of their souls to him in well doing, as unto a faithful Creator**. (1 Peter 4:12-19)

Notice that the baptism of fire is a fiery trial of persecution of Christians. 1 Peter 4:12-19 makes it clear that this persecution is a "judgment" that begins at the "house of God." Christians suffer according to the "will of God." Jesus himself refers to the baptism by fire in Luke 12:50. This reference to another baptism is obviously not a reference to a baptism of water, but rather a baptism of fire, his crucifixion.

Jesus first states that he has come to send fire on the earth and then refers to his baptism of fire (crucifixion), which will be the catalyst for the subsequent persecutions of his church. "**I am come to send fire on the earth**; and what will I, if it be already kindled? But **I have a baptism to be baptized with**; and how am I straitened till it be accomplished!" (Luke 12:49-50) In fact Jesus tells James and John, the sons of Zebedee that they will in fact be baptized with the baptism with which Jesus would be baptized.

> They said unto him, Grant unto us that we may sit, one on thy right hand, and the other on thy left hand, in thy glory. But Jesus said unto them, Ye know not what ye ask: can ye drink of the cup that I drink of? and be baptized with the baptism that I am baptized with? And they said unto him, We

can. And Jesus said unto them, **Ye shall indeed drink of the cup that I drink of; and with the baptism that I am baptized withal shall ye be baptized**: But to sit on my right hand and on my left hand is not mine to give; but it shall be given to them for whom it is prepared." (Mark 10:37-40)

We are partakers of the sufferings of Christ. Why must we endure the fiery trials of suffering? He stated that we would be persecuted for our faith in him. Jesus explained in John 15:

I am the true vine, and my Father is the husbandman. **Every branch in me that beareth not fruit he taketh away: and every branch that beareth fruit, he purgeth it, that it may bring forth more fruit.** Now ye are clean through the word which I have spoken unto you. Abide in me, and I in you. As the branch cannot bear fruit of itself, except it abide in the vine; no more can ye, except ye abide in me. I am the vine, ye *are* the branches: He that abideth in me, and I in him, the same bringeth forth much fruit: for without me ye can do nothing. **If a man abide not in me, he is cast forth as a branch, and is withered; and men gather them, and cast them into the fire, and they are burned.** If ye abide in me, and my words abide in you, ye shall ask what ye will, and it shall be done unto you. Herein is my Father glorified, that ye bear much fruit; so shall ye be my disciples. As the Father hath loved me, so have I loved you: continue ye in my love. If ye keep my commandments, ye shall abide in my love; even as I have kept my Father's commandments, and abide in his love. These things have I spoken unto you, that my joy might remain in you, and that your joy might be full. This is my commandment, That ye love one another, as I have loved you. Greater love hath no man than this, that a man lay down his life for his friends. Ye are my friends, if ye do whatsoever I command you. Henceforth I call you not servants; for the servant knoweth not what his lord doeth: but I have called you friends; for all things that I have heard of my Father I have made known unto you. **Ye have not chosen me, but I have chosen you, and ordained you, that ye should go and bring forth fruit, and that your fruit should remain: that whatsoever ye shall ask of the Father in my name, he may give it you.** These things I command you, that ye love one another. If the world hate you, ye know that it hated me before it hated you. If ye were of the world, the world would love his own: but because ye are not of the world, but I have chosen you out of the world, therefore the world hateth you. Remember the word that I said unto you, **The servant is not greater than his lord. If they have persecuted me, they will also persecute you**; if they have kept my saying, they will keep yours also. But all these things will they do unto you for my name's sake, because they know not him that sent me." (John 15:1-21)

Jesus purges the branches through suffering so that they will bear fruit. However there are those branches that bear no fruit. They are the branches that wither under the fire of Christian trials. Jesus explains this point in the parable of the sower:

Hear ye therefore the parable of the sower. When any one heareth the word of the kingdom, and understandeth it not, then cometh the wicked one, and catcheth away that which was sown in his heart. This is he which received seed by the way side. But he that received the seed into stony places, the same is he that heareth the word, and anon with joy receiveth it; Yet hath he not root in himself, but dureth for a while: **for when tribulation or persecution ariseth because of the word, by and by he is offended**. He also that received seed among the thorns is he that heareth the word; and the care of this world, and the deceitfulness of riches, choke the word, and he becometh unfruitful. But he that received seed into the good ground is he that heareth the word, and understandeth it; which also beareth fruit, and bringeth forth, some an hundredfold, some sixty, some thirty." (Matthew 13:18-23)

The apostle Paul saw this very thing happen, and he named names:

This thou knowest, that all they which are in Asia be turned away from me; of whom are Phygellus and Hermogenes. The Lord give mercy unto the house of Onesiphorus; for he oft refreshed me, and was not ashamed of my chain: But, when he was in Rome, he sought me out very diligently, and found me. The Lord grant unto him that he may find mercy of the Lord in that day: and in how many things he ministered unto me at Ephesus, thou knowest very well. (2 Timothy 1:15-18)

Did Paul suffer loss? Yes, the three years he spent in Asia being beaten and falsely accused resulted in all turning away from him. Not only were Phygellus and Hermogenes losses to him, but also Demas. "For **Demas hath forsaken me**, having loved this present world, and is departed unto Thessalonica; Crescens to Galatia, Titus unto Dalmatia." (2 Timothy 4:10) Demas was earlier described by Paul as his fellow laborer in Christ. "Marcus,

Aristarchus, **Demas**, Lucas, **my fellowlabourers**." (Philemon 1:24) Paul's loss was according to God's will. Paul explains earlier in 2 Timothy:

> Be not thou therefore ashamed of the testimony of our Lord, nor of me his prisoner: but **be thou partaker of the afflictions of the gospel according to the power of God; Who hath saved us, and called *us* with an holy calling, not according to our works, but according to his own purpose and grace, which was given us in Christ Jesus before the world began,** (2 Timothy 1:8-9)

The persecution and loss that Paul suffered was according to the will of God, who purposed it before the world was created. Paul made the important point that he was called to a holy calling of spreading the gospel not according to his works but according to God's "own purpose and grace."

Some people seem to have lost sight that not all references to rewards and losses in the Bible are references to eternal rewards and losses. Some of the rewards and losses are rewards and losses during our temporal life on earth. For example: "But thou, when thou prayest, enter into thy closet, and when thou hast shut thy door, pray to thy Father which is in secret; and thy Father which seeth in secret shall **reward thee openly**." (Matthew 6:6) The open reward is a clear reference to a reward during our temporal existence on earth.

We saw how Paul suffered loss. However, what does Paul say is his reward? In 1 Corinthians 9 he tells us what is his reward. First, he states that he has no reason to Glory. Second, he states that his reward is preaching the gospel without charge. He states that the preaching of the gospel without charge is its own reward!

> **For though I preach the gospel, I have nothing to glory of**: for necessity is laid upon me; yea, woe is unto me, if I preach not the gospel! **For if I do this thing willingly, I have a reward**: but if against my will, a dispensation of the gospel is committed unto me. **What is my reward then? Verily that, when I preach the gospel, I may make the gospel of Christ without charge, that I abuse not my power in the gospel. For though I be free from all men, yet have I made myself servant unto all, that I might gain the more."** (1 Corinthians 9:16-19)

How could the preaching itself be a reward? Because it is Christ who determines the increase. Whether someone comes to the knowledge of Christ is not up to Paul, it is up to Christ. Therefore, the only thing of which Paul can make certain is that he faithfully preaches the word of God. If he preaches the word faithfully and accurately, then the preaching will bear fruit.

However, as Jesus pointed out in the parable of the sower in Matthew 13, not all who seem to follow Christ have the true faith of Christ. Christ is not only the object of our faith he is the very source of our faith. We are dead in trespasses and sin such that Jesus must supply the faith for our salvation. "And you hath he quickened, who were dead in trespasses and sins." (Ephesians 2:1) Everything for our salvation is supplied by and through Christ. **Our faith in Christ is the faith of Christ**. *See e.g.*, Romans 3:22; Galatians 3:22; Revelation 14:12.

> Knowing that a man is not justified by the works of the law, but by the **faith of Jesus Christ**, even we have believed in Jesus Christ, that we might be justified by the **faith of Christ**, and not by the works of the law: for by the works of the law shall no flesh be justified. (Galatians 2:16)

Our salvation is all of Christ. Jesus is the **"author and finisher of our faith."** Hebrews 12:2. That means he originates, creates, and establishes our faith. He does not then leave us to our own devices. Jesus then preserves us in him forever. Our salvation is truly by his grace through faith, it is none of our own, it is all of Christ.

> **But God, who is rich in mercy, for his great love wherewith he loved us, Even when we were dead in sins, hath quickened us together with Christ, (<u>by grace ye are saved</u>;)** And hath raised *us* up together, and made *us* sit together in heavenly places in Christ Jesus: That in the ages to come he might shew the exceeding riches of his grace in his kindness toward us through Christ Jesus. **For by grace are ye saved through faith; and that not of yourselves: it is the gift of God:** Not of works, lest any man should boast. For we are his workmanship, created in Christ Jesus unto good works, which God hath before ordained that we should walk in them. (Ephesians 2:4-10) (emphasis added)

Our calling by Christ is not according to any merit or works we have done. "Who hath saved us, and called us with an holy calling, **not according to our works, but according to his own purpose and grace**, which was given us in Christ Jesus before the world began," (2 Timothy 1:9) As with our salvation, so also our very calling is not based upon some merits through works we have done on earth. Our calling to preach the gospel is according to his purpose and grace. In fact, Paul states clearly in 2 Timothy that we all receive a crown of righteousness. How then can some lose any of their heavenly blessings if we all receive a crown of righteousness that is from Christ? "Henceforth there is laid up for me a **crown of righteousness**, which the Lord, the righteous judge, shall give me at that day: **and not to me only, but**

unto all them also that love his appearing." (2 Timothy 4:8)

Let us take a closer look at 1 Corinthians 3 in context. We see that the topic is the church. Early in the chapter, Paul makes the point that the laborers in preaching the gospel and building the church are laborers with God! Not only that, the laborers are also the plants upon which God is husbanding. That is, the members of the church (gold, silver, precious stones) are also working to add more gold, silver, precious stones. "We are of God: he that knoweth God heareth us; he that is not of God heareth not us. Hereby know we the spirit of truth, and the spirit of error." (1John 4:6) However, without Christ the workers can do nothing and so Christ is right alongside them guiding the work. Christians are laboring with God, and Jesus is the good shepherd, shepherding us along.

As explained in Ephesians 2, whatever good we do is preordained by God and performed by Jesus Christ through us. We have no reason to boast and there is no eternal reward for any of our good works because our salvation is not by works but by the grace of God. Even our very faith is from God. That is why Paul stated that he had nothing to glory about. "For though I preach the gospel, I have nothing to glory of: for necessity is laid upon me; yea, woe is unto me, if I preach not the gospel!" 1 Corinthians 9:16. Jesus drove home the point when he stated: "So likewise ye, when ye shall have done all those things which are commanded you, say, We are unprofitable servants: we have done that which was our duty to do." (Luke 17:10)

Consequently, if persons come to the knowledge of Christ and are saved due to the preaching of the gospel, that is due to the work of Christ. There is not some added blessing to be received by the preacher in heaven because the gospel they preached was effectual. The glory for saving the soul goes to God and God alone. "So then neither is he that planteth any thing, neither he that watereth; but God that giveth the increase." (1 Corinthians

3:7)

Our blessing in heaven is not based upon some debt owed to us for works done on earth. Our blessing in heaven is based completely on the mercy and grace of God. Read again what God states: "For by grace are ye saved through faith; and that not of yourselves: **it is the gift of God: Not of works**, lest any man should boast." (Ephesians 2:8-9)

The topic of 1 Corinthians 3 is the church, and the foundation of the church is Christ. The issue in 1 Corinthians 3 is whether the spiritual building being built is made up of true Christians. The wood, hay, and stubble seems to be those who fall away during the fiery trials Peter mentioned in 1 Peter 4.

The preachers of the gospel will suffer loss of the pretended members of the church who fall away (wood, hay, and stubble), but the preachers themselves will be saved. However, they will go through the same fiery trials that caused the false Christians to fall away, but the true Christians will remain as gold, silver, precious stones. The passage makes clear that fire will try every man's work. What work is that? It is the body of the church, the foundation of which is Christ. The product of the work of preaching the gospel will be gold, silver, and precious stones (true Christians) and wood, hay, and stubble (false Christians).

The true Christians will persevere through the fiery trials of the persecutions suffered by Christians, however, the counterfeit Christians will wilt under the heat and fall away. The loss mentioned in 1 Corinthians 3 has nothing to do with loss of eternal blessings in heaven, it is the loss of the false brethren (the wood, hay, stubble).

> I have planted, Apollos watered; but God gave the increase. So then **neither is he that planteth any thing, neither he that watereth; but God that**

giveth the increase. **Now he that planteth and he that watereth <u>are one</u>:** and every man shall receive his own reward **according to his own labour**. For **we are labourers together with God: ye are God's husbandry, ye are God's building.** According to the grace of God which is given unto me, as a wise masterbuilder, I have laid the foundation, and another buildeth thereon. But let every man take heed how he buildeth thereupon. For **other foundation can no man lay than that is laid, which is Jesus Christ**. Now if any man build upon this foundation gold, silver, precious stones, wood, hay, stubble; Every man's work shall be made manifest: for the day shall declare it, because **it shall be revealed by fire**; and the <u>**fire shall try every man's work**</u> of what sort it is. If any man's work abide which he hath built thereupon, he shall receive a reward. If any man's work shall be burned, he shall suffer loss: but **<u>he himself shall be saved; yet so as by fire</u>. <u>Know ye not that ye are the temple of God</u>**, and that the Spirit of God dwelleth in you? If any man defile the temple of God, him shall God destroy; for **<u>the temple of God is holy, which temple ye are</u>**. Let no man deceive himself. If any man among you seemeth to be wise in this world, let him become a fool, that he may be wise. For the wisdom of this world is foolishness with God. For it is written, He taketh the wise in their own craftiness. And again, The Lord knoweth the thoughts of the wise, that they are vain. **Therefore let no man glory in men. For all things are yours; Whether Paul, or Apollos, or Cephas, or the world, or life, or death, or things present, or things to come; all are yours; And ye are Christ's; and Christ** *is* **God's.** (1 Corinthians 3:6-23)

1 Corinthians 3:6-23 clearly refers to the temple of the Lord. The wood, hay, and stubble are those who do not truly belong as part of the temple, whereas the gold, silver, and precious stones are the true Christians who make up the body of Christ. All Christians corporately are the temple of the Lord. **"Ye also, as lively stones**, are built up a spiritual house, an holy priesthood, to offer up spiritual sacrifices, acceptable to God by Jesus Christ." (1Peter 2:5)

The fiery trials suffered by Christians ultimately end with glory at the judgment seat of Christ. "That the **trial of your faith**, being much more precious than of gold that perisheth, though it be **tried with fire**, might be found unto praise and honour and glory at the appearing of Jesus Christ:" (1Peter 1:7)

> Now therefore ye are no more strangers and foreigners, but fellowcitizens with the saints, and of the household of God; And are built upon the foundation of the apostles and prophets, Jesus Christ himself being the chief corner *stone*; In whom all the building fitly framed together groweth unto **an holy temple in the Lord: In whom ye also are builded together for an habitation of God through the Spirit.** (Ephesians 2:19-22)

The wood, hay, and stubble do not weather the fiery trials and persecutions and are burned up. This brings us right back to Matthew 3:11-12, where John the Baptist makes clear that the baptism of fire will be the way in which God will separate his wheat from the chaff. The persecutions suffered for Christ are the means by which God separates the wheat from the chaff. The chaff shall be gathered and burned up with unquenchable fire, while the wheat will be gathered and preserved in his garner.

I indeed baptize you with water unto repentance:

but he that cometh after me is mightier than I, whose shoes I am not worthy to bear: **he shall baptize you with the Holy Ghost, <u>and with fire</u>**: Whose fan *is* in his hand, **and he will throughly purge his floor, and gather his wheat into the garner; but he will burn up the chaff with unquenchable fire.** (Matthew 3:11-12)

Why would God allow persecution to come to his own chosen children? Because his strength is made perfect through our weakness. Paul explains in 2 Corinthians 12:7-10:

And lest I should be exalted above measure through the abundance of the revelations, there was given to me a thorn in the flesh, the messenger of Satan to buffet me, lest I should be exalted above measure. For this thing I besought the Lord thrice, that it might depart from me. And he said unto me, My grace is sufficient for thee: for **my strength is made perfect in weakness**. Most gladly therefore will I rather glory in my infirmities, that the power of Christ may rest upon me. Therefore I take pleasure in infirmities, in reproaches, in necessities, in persecutions, in distresses for Christ's sake: for when I am weak, then am I strong. (2 Corinthians 12:7-10)

Those who would follow Christ and live the gospel will suffer persecution, just as did Paul. "Persecutions, afflictions, which came unto me at Antioch, at Iconium, at Lystra; what persecutions I endured: but out of them all the Lord delivered me. Yea, and **all that will live godly in Christ Jesus shall suffer persecution**." (2 Timothy 3:11-12) We must rely totally on Christ for our strength and to deliver us if it is his will. We are children of God and heirs of his glory. The sufferings of this world do not compare to the glory that will be revealed in us.

> And if children, then heirs; heirs of God, and joint–heirs with Christ; if so be that we suffer with him, that we may be also glorified together. For I reckon that the sufferings of this present time are not worthy to be compared with the glory which shall be revealed in us. (Romans 8:17-18)

We look forward, beyond our sufferings, to the perfection that God has awaiting us in eternal glory. Since we will be "perfect" in heavenly glory, we will not lack any rewards, because being perfect by definition means we will be completely pure, correct in every detail, and entirely without any shortcomings. This is done, not by our works, but rather by God imputing the perfection of Christ to us.

> Whom resist stedfast in the faith, knowing that the same afflictions are accomplished in your brethren that are in the world. **But the God of all grace, who hath called us unto his eternal glory by Christ Jesus, after that ye have suffered a while, make you perfect, stablish, strengthen, settle you.** 1 Peter 5:9-10.

For a more thorough explanation of the error of the loss of rewards heresy, refer to this author's book, *The Anti-Gospel: The Perversion of Christ's Grace Gospel.*

16 Perfect Salvation

There is no "in between" where God sees the good and bad of Christians and the good and bad of the unbelieving heathen. It is all or nothing with God. One is either perfectly holy in God's kingdom by the imputed righteousness of Christ or he is evil according to man's fallen nature. Concerning the unregenerate man, God's view is: "They are all gone out of the way, they are together become unprofitable; there is none that doeth good, no, not one." (Romans 3:12) However, the believer is "justified:" "For all have sinned, and come short of the glory of God; Being justified freely by his grace through the redemption that is in Christ Jesus:" (Romans 3:23-24)

Works are a manifestation of our salvation; they do not earn salvation nor any rewards. Any Christian who relies on rewards in heaven for his works on earth has abandoned God's grace and instead is looking for God to pay a debt instead of relying on the mercy of God. "Now to him that worketh is the reward not reckoned of grace, but of debt. But to him that worketh not, but believeth on him that justifieth the ungodly, his faith is counted for righteousness." (Romans 4:4-5)

How then can any Christian forfeit blessings at the judgment seat of Christ? It is impossible. Jesus himself states in

John 17, that we will be "**made perfect in one**." What is the one with whom Christians are made perfect? Christians are made perfect in one with God!

What does it mean to be perfect? Open a dictionary and read the definition. Perfect means to conform absolutely to the definition or description of the ideal type; to be excellent or complete beyond practical or theoretical improvement; to be entirely without any flaws, defects or shortcomings; to be correct in every detail; to be pure and unmixed. (http://dictionary.reference.com/browse/perfect)

A Christian in heaven and in glory cannot lack anything by having blessings taken away because God has stated that Christians will be "perfect!" That is, we will be complete, beyond any improvement, without any flaws; we will not have any shortcomings.

To claim that a Christian must work to establish his perfection in heaven is to attempt to do what God has admonished against. "Are ye so foolish? having begun in the Spirit, are ye now made perfect by the flesh?" (Galatians 3:3) God, in Colossians 1, explains that God saves Christians to be presented "perfect **in** Christ Jesus." We are not perfected by works; we are perfected by our being one "in" Jesus. Jesus, in fact, orchestrates the works that are done by Christians. The labors of Christians are "according to his working."

> To whom God would make known what *is* the riches of the glory of this mystery among the Gentiles; which is Christ in you, the hope of glory: Whom we preach, warning every man, and teaching every man in all wisdom; that we may present every man **perfect in Christ Jesus**: Whereunto I also labour, striving **according to his working, which worketh in me mightily**.

(Colossians 1:27-29)

Christians are part of the spiritual assembly in heaven made up of those who have been made perfect by Christ.

> But ye are come unto mount Sion, and unto the city of the living God, the heavenly Jerusalem, and to an innumerable company of angels, To the general assembly and church of the firstborn, which are written in heaven, and to God the Judge of all, and to the **spirits of just men made perfect**, (Hebrews 12:22-23)

If we are made perfect in one with God and share in his glory, what is there lacking? The answer is nothing. Jesus states emphatically in his prayer that God has loved us as he has loved Jesus. We share in the same love, blessing, and glory with Jesus when we enter heaven. We know this because Jesus tells us in John 17:22. This is the very same glory that Christ had with the Father before he was manifest in the flesh on earth. "And now, O Father, glorify thou me with thine own self with the glory which I had with thee before the world was." (John 17:5)

God does not partially save us; God saves us to the uttermost. That means that God saves us to perfection. "Wherefore he is able also to **save them to the uttermost** that come unto God by him, seeing he ever liveth to make intercession for them." (Heb 7:25) Uttermost salvation means that God saved us completely; God saved us to the greatest extent possible. Being saved to the uttermost means that there is no blessing that we will lack and there will be no loss of rewards due to our unrighteousness.

We need not work to add to what is already perfect. We are saved perfectly by the one offering of Jesus Christ. "For by one offering he hath perfected for ever them that are sanctified." (Hebrews 10:14) To attempt to add to Jesus' one offering on the cross is to doubt his offering's sufficiency and his promise that he entirely and perfectly saved us.

Notice how in Revelation 21 God gives of the water of life "freely," and those that overcome the world inherit "all things." God gives to us "freely," and we will inherit "all things," not some things.

> And he said unto me, It is done. I am Alpha and Omega, the beginning and the end. **I will give unto him that is athirst of the fountain of the water of life freely. He that overcometh shall inherit all things**; and I will be his God, and he shall be my son. But the fearful, and unbelieving, and the abominable, and murderers, and whoremongers, and sorcerers, and idolaters, and all liars, shall have their part in the lake which burneth with fire and brimstone: which is the second death. (Re 21:6-8)

In 1 Peter 1, God states that our perfect inheritance in heaven is "incorruptible." If God says our inheritance is incorruptible, who is man to contradict him and say "oh yes it is, it can be corrupted by your failure to do good works"? We cannot by our misdeeds in the flesh corrupt our rewards in heaven. Our inheritance is not based upon the merits of what we have done, but rather on the perfect righteousness of Jesus imputed to us, and so we cannot lose our eternal gifts. We did nothing to earn them, and therefore, we can do nothing to lose them.

> Blessed be the God and Father of our Lord Jesus Christ, which according to his abundant mercy hath begotten us again unto a lively hope by the resurrection of Jesus Christ from the dead, To an **inheritance incorruptible, and undefiled**, and that fadeth not away, reserved in heaven for you," (1Peter 1:3-4)

Christians will receive a crown of glory that will never fade away at the judgment seat of Christ. "And when the chief Shepherd shall appear, ye shall receive a crown of glory that fadeth not away." (1Peter 5:4) The reason a Christian's inheritance is incorruptible and cannot fade away is that Christians are in Christ and Christ is in them. We are one with Christ and are partakers of the divine nature of Christ. "Whereby are given unto us exceeding great and precious promises: that by these ye might be partakers of the divine nature, having escaped the corruption that is in the world through lust." (2Peter 1:4)

17 Two Kinds of Works

Not only are there two kinds of faith, but there are also two kinds of works. Those that redefine justification in the book of James to mean justification before men by works do not understand that there are two kinds of works. There are those works ordained by God through faith and then there are those other works that flow from man's will. These charlatan preachers think that the works that Paul is discussing in Romans 4:1-5 are the same works that James is talking about. They are not. Read carefully what Paul says:

> What shall we say then that Abraham our father, as pertaining to the **flesh**, hath found? For if Abraham were justified by works, he hath whereof to glory; but not before God. For what saith the scripture? Abraham believed God, and it was counted unto him for righteousness. Now to him that worketh is the reward not reckoned of grace, but of **debt**. But to him that worketh not, but believeth on him that justifieth the ungodly, his faith is counted for righteousness.(Romans 4:1-5)

Paul is not contradicting James. Paul in Romans 4:1-5 and James in chapter 2 are addressing two different kinds of works.

Paul is explaining that Abraham was NOT justified by the works of the flesh. He leads off with: "What shall we say then that Abraham our father, as pertaining to the **flesh**, hath found?" He makes the point that Abraham's righteousness was NOT from the works of the flesh. Abraham was NOT justified by works. But wait a minute, didn't James say that works justified Abraham? He did. Isn't that a contradiction? No. And that is because in Romans Paul is talking about the works of the **flesh**. Whereas James is talking about the **works of faith**.

The works of faith are those works ordained and performed by God through the believer that perfect his faith. They are the result of faith. That perfect faith justifies the believer. In contrast, works of the flesh cannot ever justify the believer. Paul explains that a person who works in the flesh is looking for a reward. "Now to him that worketh is the reward not reckoned of grace, but of debt." But the works born of faith are the fruit of salvation; they do not earn salvation; they are not for a reward. Salvation is a gift of God and not a reward for good works. Good works flow from salvation. That is what James is saying. Good works do not earn salvation. That is what Paul is saying.

The good works follow salvation; they do not earn salvation. Works do not save us. As Paul explained in his letter to Titus:

> Not by works of righteousness which we have done, but according to his mercy he saved us, by the washing of regeneration, and renewing of the Holy Ghost;" (Titus 3:5)

Paul and James agree. The passage in Romans 4:1-4 is making a point that works do not save. But Paul explains later in Chapters 6 and 8 of Romans that works follow salvation. That is the point being made by James, Chapter 2. Paul and James do not contradict one another. They are in complete agreement.

Romans 4:1-5: Good works do not earn salvation.

James 2: Good works are the fruit of salvation.

Many people do not understand that basic gospel concept. I have had "Christians" tell me that "works are works,"[62] meaning by that statement that there is no difference between the fleshly works spoken about by Paul that can never save and the works spoken of by James that are the fruit of salvation. They do not understand the distinction between the good works that are the fruit of salvation and the ineffectual works men do to earn salvation. Paul succinctly states that we are saved by Jesus Christ so "that we should bring forth fruit unto God." Romans 7:4.

For example, the eminent "Christian" theologian Zane Hodges states that works are utterly irrelevant to salvation. He interprets Paul to say that whether the works precede salvation or come after salvation, they are completely separate from faith. According to Hodges, faith can have nothing to do with works. Hodges claims the following:

> But at bottom, Paul believed two very basic things. These were: (1) God, apart from man's works, justifies the one who believes in Jesus; and (2) the cross is the basis for this justification and shows it to be a fully righteous act. Here it is important to say that for Paul these are absolute realities totally independent of anything man does before or after faith. There is no basis whatsoever in Paul's letters to connect human works with justification by faith no matter when these works are performed. Whether done before or after conversion, they remain works (i.e., erga = "deeds" or "actions"). The distinction drawn by some writers between "works done to attain favor with God" and "works done out of faith or gratitude" is non-existent in the

Pauline material. This alleged distinction is a theological fiction.[63]

Hodges' position is irreconcilable with the gospel, particularly chapter 2 of James and chapters 6 and 8 of Romans. That is why Hodges had to redefine justification by works spoken of by James to only refer to the justification before men and not by God. Hodges completely dismisses any connection between faith and works. He conflates the heresy of works meriting salvation with the gospel theme that faith will bear fruit. Hodges seems to think that bearing fruit somehow means that the good works "contribute" to salvation, which is not what James is saying. Hodges seems to pit Paul against James and in doing so is putting words in James' mouth. Hodges states:

> For Paul, "good works," whether done under or apart from the Mosaic Law, cannot contribute to our justification. To say that somehow they do contribute would really amount to a denial of the simple fact that God justifies the person who has faith in Jesus. In that case God would be justifying only the person who has faith plus works, not a person who just has faith. No matter how this idea is articulated, it contradicts Paul's fundamental idea that justification is "apart from works" (v 28; see 4:6). Furthermore, to say that "our (post-conversion) works" somehow vindicate God's justification is a denial of the adequacy of the cross for that purpose. The famous statement that "we are saved by faith alone, but not by a faith that is alone" is a Reformation idea, not a Pauline one. This idea can be found nowhere in Paul's writings.[64]

Hodges, and his ilk, eschew the idea that dead faith cannot save. Hodges claims that faith that has no works is saving faith. He claims that is what Paul meant.[65]

Hodges claims that grace and works are polar opposites and can have no connection.

> But in Paul's writings works do not have any connection whatsoever with the truth of justification. For Paul grace and works are opposites. He will later say in this very epistle: "But if it is by grace, it is no longer by works, otherwise grace is no longer grace. But if it is by works, it is no longer grace, otherwise work is no longer work" (Rom 11:6). This is perfectly plain, and theologians have wasted their time trying to qualify, revise, or reinterpret Paul's lucid concept. According to Paul, when you mix faith and works you change the basic nature of both.[66]

Hodges does not understand what Paul was saying in Romans 11:6. Paul was saying that salvation is "by" grace; and that salvation is not "by" works. He was making the point that our works cannot save us. Our salvation is all "by" grace. Paul is not saying anything in that passage about the works that flow from saving faith.

Jesus was pretty clear in saying that faith without works is not saving faith: "Not every one that saith unto me, Lord, Lord, shall enter into the kingdom of heaven; but he that doeth the will of my Father which is in heaven." (Matthew 7:21) When you read that statement in context, it is a statement that punctuates his dissertation on good fruits and evil fruits.

> Beware of false prophets, which come to you in sheep's clothing, but inwardly they are ravening wolves. Ye shall know them by their fruits. Do men gather grapes of thorns, or figs of thistles?

Even so every good tree bringeth forth good fruit; but a corrupt tree bringeth forth evil fruit. A good tree cannot bring forth evil fruit, neither can a corrupt tree bring forth good fruit. **Every tree that bringeth not forth good fruit is hewn down, and cast into the fire.** Wherefore by their fruits ye shall know them. (Matthew 7:15-20)

It is in the very next verse that Jesus says that "[n]ot every one that saith unto me, Lord, Lord, shall enter into the kingdom of heaven; but he that doeth the will of my Father which is in heaven." (Matthew 7:21) Jesus is talking about salvation here. Thus, all those who bring forth good fruit are saved. There is only good fruit and bad fruit. There is no in-between category that is neither good fruit nor bad fruit, as some preachers would have their followers believe. They preach that a person can get into heaven without any good works. They can have faith without works. Jesus said that "every tree that bringeth NOT forth good fruit is hewn down and cast into the fire." To avoid the fire you must have good fruit, which can only come by the grace of God through saving faith in Jesus Christ.

If you are in Christ, you will bear good fruit. Faith without works is dead. But in the minds of many preachers, any connection between works and faith corrupts the concept of salvation by faith alone. They must categorize James' reference to "justification by works," as not James expressing that true saving faith has works, but rather as justification before men by works. We saw that in an earlier chapter with the preaching and writings of MacArthur, Fortner, Hodges, Anderson, and Gill. It seems that they think that to say that saving faith comes with works (as James clearly states) in some way means that one is requiring works to be added to the finished work of Christ. And so they steer clear of associating saving faith with works. They got twisted in their cleverness and lost sight of the simple message of the gospel.

Thus, to them, faith without works is ONLY dead faith before man and NOT dead faith before God because according to them, faith with works ONLY justify us before men and NOT God. Mind you, James 2 teaches that we are justified in the sight of God by faith, but that faith, to be true faith, will have good works. There is no such thing as fruitless saving faith.

James 2:18 says: "Yea, a man may say, Thou hast faith, and I have works: shew me thy faith without thy works, and I will shew thee my faith by my works." and James 2:24 says: "Ye see then how that by works a man is justified, and not by faith only." James explained what he means: "For as the body without the spirit is dead, so faith without works is dead also." (James 2:26)

James is saying, that we are saved by faith, the kind of faith that has works. That is faith that comes "with" works. We are saved by the kind of faith that comes "with" works. James is not saying that works justify a man. He is saying that faith that has no fruit is not saving faith. "Faith without works is dead." James 2:20.

18 Paul Affirms James

In the letter to the Galatians, Paul says that same thing that James said. Paul says that the fruit of the Spirit are the works of love. If one has the Holy Spirit in him he will walk in that Spirit. When Paul speaks of our "walk," he is saying the same thing that James is saying when James uses the word "works." Paul's "walk" is James' "works." James states that saving faith will have the works of love; Paul is saying that a person who has saving faith will walk in love accordingly.

> Be ye therefore followers of God, as dear children; And **walk in love**, as Christ also hath loved us, and hath given himself for us an offering and a sacrifice to God for a sweetsmelling savour." (Ephesians 5:1-2)

The faith and the works are both gifts of the Holy Spirit that indwells the believer. "The just shall live by faith." Romans 1:17. Paul means that the believer will walk in faith and in the Spirit that indwells the believer. In his letter to the Colossians Paul reveals that the walk he is talking about is **"being fruitful in every good work."** The walk of Paul is the same works spoken of by James and the fruit spoken of by Jesus in John 15:5.

That ye might walk worthy of the Lord unto all pleasing, being fruitful in every good work, and increasing in the knowledge of God." (Colossians 1:10)

Paul explains: "As ye have therefore received Christ Jesus the Lord, so **walk ye in him**." Colossians 2:6. Notice we are to walk "in" Christ Jesus. That is a Spiritual walk. "For ye were sometimes darkness, but now are ye light in the Lord: **walk as children of light**:" (Ephesians 5:8) While we are saved by God's Grace through faith in Jesus Christ, and that faith is a gift from God, and we are not saved by works, **"we are his workmanship, created in Christ Jesus unto good works, which God hath before ordained that we should walk in them."** (Ephesians 2:10)

If a believer does not walk in the Spirit he is not saved. Paul is reiterating what James said. "Faith without works is dead." James 2:20. Indeed, Paul says that it is "not the hearers of the law are just before God, but the doers of the law shall be justified." (Romans 2:13) That sounds very much like what James said when he explained: "Ye see then how that by works a man is justified, and not by faith only." (James 2:24)

What does James mean by people being justified by "works?" And what does Paul mean by "doers of the law" being justified? James explains that his works are the fruit of his faith. "Yea, a man may say, Thou hast faith, and I have works: shew me thy faith without thy works, and I will shew thee my faith by my works." (James 2:18) God wants doers of his gospel not just hearers. "But be ye doers of the word, and not hearers only, deceiving your own selves." (James 1:22) Paul explains the same principle, that "doers of the law" are justified by God through saving faith, which necessarily causes them to walk in the Spirit:

This I say then, Walk in the Spirit, and ye shall not fulfil the lust of the flesh. For the flesh lusteth against the Spirit, and the Spirit against the flesh: and these are contrary the one to the other: so that ye cannot do the things that ye would. But if ye be led of the Spirit, ye are not under the law. Now the works of the flesh are manifest, which are these; Adultery, fornication, uncleanness, lasciviousness, Idolatry, witchcraft, hatred, variance, emulations, wrath, strife, seditions, heresies, Envyings, murders, drunkenness, revellings, and such like: of the which I tell you before, as I have also told you in time past, that **they which do such things shall not inherit the kingdom of God. But the fruit of the Spirit is love, joy, peace, longsuffering, gentleness, goodness, faith, Meekness, temperance: against such there is no law. And they that are Christ's have crucified the flesh with the affections and lusts. If we live in the Spirit, let us also walk in the Spirit.** (Galatians 5:16-25)

James said that faith that has not fruit (i.e., love) is dead. Paul says that the fruit of the Spirit is "love, joy, peace, longsuffering, gentleness, goodness, faith, Meekness, and temperance." Paul says that if we live in the Spirit of Christ **"let us also walk in the Spirit."** Walking is doing works. Notice, though, that Paul makes a statement of the status of those in Christ. "[T]hey that are Christ's have crucified the flesh with the affections and lusts." That is a statement of fact. Paul is saying that those who are in Christ will bear the fruit of their salvation by walking in the Spirit because they are dead to the desires of the flesh which were crucified with Christ on the cross. He also is saying that those who walk in the flesh "shall not inherit the kingdom of God." That is the same thing that James is saying. Faith without the works of the Spirit is dead and "shall not inherit the kingdom of God."

Notice how Paul explains that all of the fruits are from the Spirit of God. They are coming from God. Paul says, flat out, a statement of fact, that **"they that are Christ's have crucified the flesh."** The flesh is now dead. Thus, the works that are being done are NOT being done by the flesh, they are NOT by the will of man, but by the will of God. *See* John 1:13. The works are being done by the Spirit of God that lives in the believer.

Paul in Romans 8:1 explains that those who are the saved elect and are in Christ "walk NOT after the flesh, but after the Spirit." That is not an admonition to walk after the Spirit. It is a statement of fact. That means that the saved will do the good works that are the fruit of saving faith that James spoke of in James, Chapter 2. Paul and James are saying the same thing.

> There is therefore now no condemnation to them which are in Christ Jesus, **who walk not after the flesh, but after the Spirit.** (Romans 8:1)

Paul builds on that theme in Romans 8:4 by asserting further "[t]hat the righteousness of the law might be fulfilled in us, who walk not after the flesh, but after the Spirit." (Romans 8:4) Again, we find that those who walk after the Spirit do so in perfect righteousness, which can be only done by God through the Holy Spirit that is in us. It is Jesus Christ working the works of God through us by the Holy Spirit that indwells us. "The steps of a good man are ordered by the Lord: and he delighteth in his way." Psalm 37:23.

In Romans 8:4, Paul is stating a fact of the gospel. Those who are saved will walk in perfect righteousness "after the Spirit." When Paul talks about walking he is talking about works. He is talking about the fruit of salvation. This confirms what James was saying. True faith will bear the fruit of that faith because "faith without works is dead." James 2:20.

Paul continues with his confirmation of James in Romans 8:9-10. Paul makes the statement that the saved elect "are not in the flesh, but in the Spirit." It is a statement of fact. It is the condition of a person who has genuine faith from God in Jesus Christ. And that can only be the case, Paul explains, "if so be that the Spirit of God dwell in you." If a person seems to have faith, but he is not the elect of God, and "have not the Spirit of Christ" and instead has the faith without works (i.e., the faith of devils), "he is none of his." He is not saved. But if a person has the faith "of" Jesus Christ (Romans 3:22; James 2:1) he has living faith and will bear the fruit of that living faith.

> But ye are not in the flesh, but in the Spirit, if so be that the Spirit of God dwell in you. Now if any man have not the Spirit of Christ, he is none of his. And if Christ be in you, the body is dead because of sin; but the Spirit is life because of righteousness. (Romans 8:9-10)

Those who are the elect of Jesus Christ are led by his Holy Spirit and will bear the fruit of that leading. "For as many as are led by the Spirit of God, they are the sons of God." (Romans 8:14) Paul explains how a saved person walks in newness of life according to the likeness of Christ. That is not an exaggeration. That is a statement of fact.

> Know ye not, that so many of us as were baptized into Jesus Christ were baptized into his death? Therefore we are buried with him by baptism into death: that like as Christ was raised up from the dead by the glory of the Father, even so **we also should walk in newness of life.** For if we have been planted together in the likeness of his death, **we shall be also in the likeness of his resurrection.** (Romans 6:3-5)

There are two things going on upon being born again from above. Our former self is crucified with Christ. Our new self is raised with Christ. We now walk by the faith of Christ in that "newness of life." Unseen to us, but yet very real, is the spiritual truth that our old man that was enslaved to sin is now set free from that sin. We can now live for Christ, which was an impossibility without the election by God's grace through faith in Jesus Christ. We now "live with him." That is we walk after his Spirit. Our faith bears the fruit of that new walk.

> Knowing this, that our old man is crucified with him, that the body of sin might be destroyed, that henceforth we should not serve sin. For he that is dead is freed from sin. **Now if we be dead with Christ, we believe that we shall also live with him**: Knowing that Christ being raised from the dead dieth no more; death hath no more dominion over him. For in that he died, he died unto sin once: but in that he liveth, he liveth unto God. Likewise reckon ye also yourselves to be dead indeed unto sin, but alive unto God through Jesus Christ our Lord. (Romans 6:6-11)

We are no longer obeying the lusts of the flesh. Our bodies are no longer instruments of unrighteousness. Paul states a fact. We are now freed from sin and have thus become "servants of righteousness." That is our new condition. Paul says that we are now free from sin, and are servants to God; thus, "**ye have your fruit unto holiness, and the end everlasting life.**" That means our saving faith that brings us everlasting life, necessarily, will have fruit. It is a statement of fact. There can be no fruitless faith. It is another way of saying what James said: "faith without works is dead." James 2:20. We were made free by God from sin. We are given the gift of eternal life freely by God's grace through faith. That faith will bear fruit. Paul explains:

Being then made free from sin, ye became the servants of righteousness. I speak after the manner of men because of the infirmity of your flesh: for as ye have yielded your members servants to uncleanness and to iniquity unto iniquity; even so now **yield your members servants to righteousness unto holiness.** For when ye were the servants of sin, ye were free from righteousness. What fruit had ye then in those things whereof ye are now ashamed? for the end of those things is death. **But now being made free from sin, and become servants to God, ye have your fruit unto holiness, and the end everlasting life.** For the wages of sin is death; but the gift of God is eternal life through Jesus Christ our Lord. (Romans 6:18-23)

Let us look at James 2:14 and see what Paul thinks about what James said. "What doth it profit, my brethren, though a man say he hath faith, and have not works? can faith save him?" James 2:14. Paul answers that question with an emphatic, No! In Romans 8:4 Paul explains that the righteousness of the law is fulfilled in us by our faith in Christ. Those who have faith in Christ walk after the Spirit of Christ that is in us. The "walk" to which Paul refers is what James calls "works." That is our genuine faith has works. "That the righteousness of the law might be fulfilled in us, **who walk not after the flesh, but after the Spirit.**" Romans 8:4.

Paul explains in Romans 8:14 that once one is saved they are then led by the Spirit of God. That leading is unto good works. "For as many as are **led by the Spirit of God**, they are the sons of God." Romans 8:14. Paul explains in Romans 8:5-6 that those who do not walk after the Spirit, that is they do not have Jesus inspired works, are walking after the flesh. Such flesh walking does not count as the good works that James describes in James, Chapter 2. It is the mind that has been transformed by Christ that causes us to mind the things of the Spirit. "For they that are after the flesh do mind the things of the flesh; **but they that are after the Spirit the things of the Spirit**. For to be carnally minded is death; but to be spiritually minded is life and peace." Romans 8:5-6. We walk according to our Spirit led mind. Paul explains that "they that are in the flesh cannot please God." Romans 8:8.

That is what James meant when he said: "Yea, a man may say, Thou hast faith, and I have works: shew me thy faith without thy works, and I will shew thee my faith by my works." (James 2:18) That is the concept that James was conveying when he stated:

> But wilt thou know, O vain man, that faith without works is dead? Was not Abraham our father justified by works, when he had offered Isaac his son upon the altar? Seest thou how faith wrought with his works, and by works was faith made perfect? And the scripture was fulfilled which saith, Abraham believed God, and it was imputed unto him for righteousness: and he was called the Friend of God. Ye see then how that by works a man is justified, and not by faith only. (James 2:20-24)

Paul comes alongside James and repeats that concept. Paul states:

> And the father of circumcision to them who are not of the circumcision only, but **who also walk in the steps of that faith of our father Abraham**, which he had being yet uncircumcised. (Romans 4:12)

Paul is saying that just as Abraham was saved by faith and his works were the fruit of that faith, so also, those that have the faith of Abraham are saved by that same faith and will have the fruit of that faith. Paul uses the words "walk in the steps of that faith of our farther Abraham" to describe the works to which James refers. James uses the word "works" where Paul uses the word "walk" to mean the fruit of saving faith.

Paul reiterates that theme in his letter to the Galatians. "This I say then, **Walk in the Spirit**, and ye shall not fulfil the lust of the flesh." (Galatians 5:16) The walk in the Spirit is the walk according to the leading of the Holy Spirit. It is the works born of saving faith to which James referred. The walk is orchestrated by God. Paul explains that reality in his second letter to the Corinthians.

> And what agreement hath the temple of God with idols? for ye are the temple of the living God; as God hath said, **I will dwell in them, and walk in them**; and I will be their God, and they shall be my people. (2 Corinthians 6:16)

God dwells in the believer through Holy Spirit and performs good works through him during his Christian walk. Believers do the will of Christ in every good work. It is God who is performing the works of the Spirit through the believer. James said regarding Abraham that "by works was faith made perfect." James 2:22. Paul affirms that point in the book of Hebrews where he explains that God makes us perfect by the good works that he performs through us.

> Now the God of peace, that brought again from the dead our Lord Jesus, that great shepherd of the sheep, through the blood of the everlasting covenant, **Make you perfect in every good work to do his will, working in you that which is wellpleasing in his sight, through Jesus Christ; to whom be glory for ever and ever. Amen."** (Hebrews 13:20-21)

19 John and Peter Affirm James and Paul

John affirms both James and Paul that faith without works is dead. Of course, they agree because the letters from Paul, James, and John were all written by God through them and God's gospel is consistent. The theme of the gospel is that a person who has the faith **"of"** Jesus Christ (Galatians 3:22) will bear the fruit of that faith. There is no such thing as a fruitless child of God. John, as did Paul, uses the word "walk" to describe what James calls "works." John explains:

> This then is the message which we have heard of him, and declare unto you, that God is light, and in him is no darkness at all. **If we say that we have fellowship with him, and walk in darkness, we lie, and do not the truth:** But if we **walk in the light**, as he is in the light, we have fellowship one with another, and the blood of Jesus Christ his Son cleanseth us from all sin. (1 John 1:5-7)

Notice that John has only two categories of walking. Walking in darkness or walking in light. You might ask, isn't there a gray area where a person is neither sinning nor doing good? The answer is no. A person who does not do good when he knows to do it is sinning. God clarifies that it is a sin for those who are given an opportunity to do good and knowingly do not do it. **"Therefore to him that knoweth to do good, and doeth it not, to him it is sin."** (James 4:17) So a person is either walking in the light or walking in darkness. One can only walk in the light by the power of the Holy Spirit who walks in them. The bottom line is that all unrighteousness of whatever sort is a sin. **"All unrighteousness is sin."** (1 John 5:17) Any time we do not show charity toward another, it is a sin. It is not a suggestion by God that we love one another, it is a command. See Matthew 22:35-40.

The difference between the saved and unsaved is that by God's grace, through faith, the saved are cleansed from **"all unrighteousness."** "If we confess our sins, he is faithful and just to forgive us our sins, and to **cleanse us from all unrighteousness**." 1 John 1:9. God sees only the righteous acts of his elect; the sins are washed clean by the blood of Jesus Christ.

> Come now, and let us reason together, saith the LORD: though your sins be as scarlet, they shall be as white as snow; though they be red like crimson, they shall be as wool. Isaiah 1:18.

God has promised to forget all the sins of his elect. **"And their sins and iniquities will I remember no more."** Hebrews 10:17. We can take God at his word. While a saved person will sin, his sins are forgiven. The other difference between the saved and unsaved is that the saved will walk according to the Spirit and only the saved are capable of doing any good works because the works are the works of Christ who works through them.

John explains that all who act righteously are born again. "If ye know that he is righteous, ye know that every one that doeth righteousness is born of him." (1 John 2:29) John is making a bold statement of fact. "Every one" who acts righteously "is" born of Jesus Christ. That, necessarily, means that no one can act righteously if they are not the saved elect of Jesus Christ. That is because all righteous acts are done by God as he works through the believer. Without Jesus Christ no one can bear fruit. The fruit are the good works flowing from saving faith.

What is this walking in the light of which John speaks? It is a walk of love. James explains: "If ye fulfil the royal law according to the scripture, Thou shalt love thy neighbour as thyself, ye do well:" (James 2:8) The royal law is that law that summarizes all the law and the prophets. Matthew 22:37-40. In his second letter, John explains that the commandment to which he repeatedly refers is simply "that we love one another." We are to walk in love for one another. To walk is to do the works of love. John, James, and Paul all have a theme in their epistles. True saving faith will bear the fruit of that salvation.

> And now I beseech thee, lady, not as though I wrote a new commandment unto thee, but that which **we had from the beginning, that we love one another. And this is love, that we walk after his commandments. This is the commandment, That, as ye have heard from the beginning, ye should walk in it.** (2 John 1:5-6)

John, in his first letter, reveals that if one knows Jesus Christ, he will keep his commandment to love one another. It is impossible to do that unless the Holy Spirit indwells and works through the elect child of God.

> My little children, these things write I unto you, that ye sin not. And if any man sin, we have an advocate with the Father, Jesus Christ the righteous: And he is the propitiation for our sins: and not for ours only, but also for the sins of the whole world. And hereby **we do know that we know him, if we keep his commandments. He**

that saith, I know him, and keepeth not his commandments, is a liar, and the truth is not in him. But whoso keepeth his word, in him verily is the love of God perfected: hereby know we that we are in him. He that saith he abideth in him ought himself also so to walk, even as he walked. (1 John 2:1-6)

Notice that John states that "he that saith, I know him, and keepeth not his commandments, is a liar, and the truth is not in him." Recall that the royal commandment is to love your neighbor as yourself. John is saying what James said when he explained that "faith without works is dead." James 2:20. John explains that if one claims he has faith but does not have the works of love that are the fruit of that faith, he is a liar. We are to walk as Jesus Christ walked. And we will do that if the Holy Spirit is in us and we are in Christ. James explains how the faith "of" Jesus Christ comes with the fruit of charity:

> What doth it profit, my brethren, though a man say he hath faith, and have not works? can faith save him? If a brother or sister be naked, and destitute of daily food, And one of you say unto them, Depart in peace, be ye warmed and filled; notwithstanding ye give them not those things which are needful to the body; what doth it profit? Even so faith, if it hath not works, is dead, being alone. Yea, a man may say, Thou hast faith, and I have works: shew me thy faith without thy works, and I will shew thee my faith by my works. Thou believest that there is one God; thou doest well: the devils also believe, and tremble. But wilt thou know, O vain man, that faith without works is dead? (James 2:14-20)

What is the end of those who claim to have faith but bear

no fruit of that faith. Jesus gives us that answer. A servant was given one talent, and hid it, and that hidden talent did not benefit anyone. That servant was described as an unprofitable servant who was cast "into outer darkness: there shall be weeping and gnashing of teeth." Matthew 25:30. Jesus explained that "every branch in me that beareth not fruit he taketh away." John 15:2. Taken away where? Jesus explains:

> I am the vine, ye are the branches: He that abideth in me, and I in him, the same bringeth forth much fruit: for without me ye can do nothing. If a man abide not in me, he is cast forth as a branch, and is withered; and men gather them, and **cast them into the fire, and they are burned.** (John 15:5-6)

Those that have dead faith are not saved. They have been marked for destruction. In his parable of the sower, Jesus explains how it can be that there are some who profess that they believe but really are lost.

> Hear ye therefore the parable of the sower. When any one heareth the word of the kingdom, and understandeth it not, then cometh the wicked one, and catcheth away that which was sown in his heart. This is he which received seed by the way side. But he that received the seed into stony places, the same is he that heareth the word, and anon with joy receiveth it; Yet hath he not root in himself, but dureth for a while: for when tribulation or persecution ariseth because of the word, by and by he is offended. He also that received seed among the thorns is he that heareth the word; and the care of this world, and the deceitfulness of riches, choke the word, and he becometh **unfruitful.** But he that received seed into the good ground is he that heareth the word,

and understandeth it; which also **beareth fruit,** and bringeth forth, some an hundredfold, some sixty, some thirty." (Matthew 13:18-23)

Notice that neither word on the stony ground nor the word sowed among the thorns bore fruit. Jesus makes the point that faith without fruit is dead. It is only the faith that bears fruit that is saving faith. Jesus explained in another parable how tares that do not offer any benefit (i.e., no fruit) are gathered and burned. In contrast, God gathers the wheat that bears the beneficial grain (i.e., fruit) into his kingdom.

> Another parable put he forth unto them, saying, The kingdom of heaven is likened unto a man which sowed good seed in his field: But while men slept, his enemy came and sowed tares among the wheat, and went his way. But when the blade was sprung up, and brought forth fruit, then appeared the tares also. So the servants of the householder came and said unto him, Sir, didst not thou sow good seed in thy field? from whence then hath it tares? He said unto them, An enemy hath done this. The servants said unto him, Wilt thou then that we go and gather them up? But he said, Nay; lest while ye gather up the tares, ye root up also the wheat with them. Let both grow together until the harvest: and in the time of harvest I will say to the reapers, **Gather ye together first the tares, and bind them in bundles to burn them: but gather the wheat into my barn."** (Matthew 13:24-30)

Indeed, it is the very theme of the gospel that God imparts the believer with saving faith, and that saving faith bears beneficial fruit. Jesus explains without equivocation that **"[n]ot every one that saith unto me, Lord, Lord, shall enter into the kingdom of heaven; but he that doeth the will of my Father which is in**

heaven." Matthew 7:21. Notice that it is the people who do the will of the Father who are saved. True faith of Christ comes with the works of Christ. The person who only professes to believe but does not do the will of the Father (i.e., has no good works) is damned to hell. Jesus is saying that same thing as James and Paul and John. "Faith without works is dead." James 2:20. Such fruitless tares were never elected by God for salvation. Jesus Christ proclaims that he never knew them. "And then will I profess unto them, I never knew you: depart from me, ye that work iniquity." Matthew 7:23.

Peter affirms James, Paul, and John. Peter explains that God has given his elect the power through his Holy Spirit necessary for a godly walk. "According as his divine power hath given unto us all things that pertain unto life and godliness, through the knowledge of him that hath called us to glory and virtue:" (2 Peter 1:3) We are imbued with the "divine nature" of God. 2 Peter 1:4. This then allows us to be free from the corruption of sin and act in love and charity toward others. 2 Peter 1:5-7. Peter punctuates his explanation with the truth that one who is imbued with the Holy Spirit of God he then will be fruitful in charity toward others.

> For if these things be in you, and abound, they make you that ye shall neither be barren nor unfruitful in the knowledge of our Lord Jesus Christ. (2 Peter 1:8)

Peter then reiterates what James, Paul, and John had said. If one does not walk in charity toward others he is "blind, and cannot see afar off, and hath forgotten that he was purged from his old sins." 2 Peter 1:9.

Peter explains that our faith and hope is in God, not our own works. We are redeemed by the precious blood of Jesus Christ. 1 Peter 1:18-19. But Peter reveals that faith by which we are saved bears fruit. That fruit is to love on another. Our fruit is closely linked to our faith. Peter explains that the Holy Spirit uses our faith to lead us to obey God and love one another. Thus, our faith bears the fruit of the good works of love.

> Who by him do believe in God, that raised him up from the dead, and gave him glory; that your faith and hope might be in God. Seeing ye have purified your souls in **obeying the truth through the Spirit unto unfeigned love of the brethren,** see that ye love one another with a pure heart fervently." (1 Peter 1:21-22)

20 The Works of Christ

It is often asked, what are the works to which James refers? James explains what he means. James explains: "My brethren, have not the faith of our Lord Jesus Christ, the Lord of glory, with respect of persons." (James 2:1) What does he mean by that? James gives a series of examples where a Christian should treat another person with love regardless of their station in life, whether they are rich and powerful or whether they are poor and impotent. James concludes by explaining that a Christian is to do the works of love toward all.

> If ye fulfil the royal law according to the scripture, **Thou shalt love thy neighbour as thyself**, ye do well: But if ye have respect to persons, ye commit sin, and are convinced of the law as transgressors. (James 2:8-9)

A few verses after that statement, James explains: "What doth it profit, my brethren, though a man say he hath faith, and have not works? can faith save him?" (James 2:14) That is when he explains that true, saving faith has works. What works? The works of love. **"Thou shalt love thy neighbour as thyself."** He concludes with the gospel message that "as the body without the spirit is dead, so faith without works is dead also." (James 2:26)

Those good works are the works of Jesus Christ performed through the believer. We are born again through the Holy Spirit as new creations in Christ Jesus to do good works ordained by God for us to walk in them. We are not saved by works, our works are the fruit of our salvation. As Paul explained:

> For by grace are ye saved through faith; and that not of yourselves: it is the gift of God: Not of works, lest any man should boast. **For we are his workmanship, created in Christ Jesus unto good works, which God hath before ordained that we should walk in them.** (Ephesians 2:8-10)

Of course, God sees all, and those works of Christ are seen by God as the works of Christ. Indeed, at the judgment seat of Christ, the only good works that are seen are the works of Christ. A believer is cloaked with the righteousness of Jesus Christ. The scriptures are clear that it is not necessary for the believer to be *de facto* righteous (in fact righteous) to be saved. Instead, Jesus imputes his righteousness to the believer, who is consequently made *de jure* righteous (legally righteous). 2 Corinthians 5:21. Christians are justified by the Lord Jesus Christ, and by virtue of having been made legally righteous, we have peace with God. Romans 5:1.

A pardon excuses a person from the penalty for a crime. However, the person pardoned is not absolved of the guilt. God does more than pardon believers; he justifies them. When a person is justified for an alleged wicked act, it means more than a pardon. Justification is a declaration that the person is absolved not only of the punishment but also of the guilt. The person justified is not subject to the punishment for the wicked act, and, in addition, he is not guilty. When the Bible declares that one is justified, though, it does not mean that the person is imparted with actual righteousness of his own because the person is, in fact, guilty of the sin. Rather, justification through Christ means that God imputes the righteousness of Christ to the believer, and thus God views the person as not guilty of the sin. It is a legal, spiritual exchange; the believer's sins are imputed to Christ, who paid the penalty for them; and Christ's righteousness is imputed to the believer.

All those who are saved will bear the fruit of good works, and that is all that God will see of the believer on judgment day. "Herein is my Father glorified, that ye bear much fruit; so shall ye be my disciples." (John 15:8) Thus, the disciples of Christ will necessarily bear much fruit. There are not two judgments; there is one judgment where both the saved (sheep) and unsaved (goats) both appear before God's judgment seat.

> When the Son of man shall come in his glory, and all the holy angels with him, then shall he sit upon the throne of his glory: And before him shall be gathered all nations: and he shall separate them one from another, as a shepherd divideth his sheep from the goats: And he shall set the **sheep on his right hand, but the goats on the left**. Then shall the King say unto them on his right hand, Come, ye blessed of my Father, **inherit the kingdom prepared for you from the foundation of the world**: For I was an hungred, and ye gave me meat: I was thirsty, and ye gave me drink: I was a stranger, and ye took me in: Naked, and ye clothed me: I was sick, and ye visited me: I was in prison, and ye came unto me. Then shall the righteous answer him, saying, Lord, when saw we thee an hungred, and fed thee? or thirsty, and gave thee drink? When saw we thee a stranger, and took thee in? or naked, and clothed thee? Or when saw we thee sick, or in prison, and came unto thee? And the King shall answer and say unto them, **Verily I say unto you, Inasmuch as ye have done it unto**

one of the least of these my brethren, ye have done it unto me. Then shall he say also unto them on the left hand, Depart from me, ye cursed, into everlasting fire, prepared for the devil and his angels: For I was an hungred, and ye gave me no meat: I was thirsty, and ye gave me no drink: I was a stranger, and ye took me not in: naked, and ye clothed me not: sick, and in prison, and ye visited me not. Then shall they also answer him, saying, Lord, when saw we thee an hungred, or athirst, or a stranger, or naked, or sick, or in prison, and did not minister unto thee? Then shall he answer them, saying, Verily I say unto you, **Inasmuch as ye did it not to one of the least of these, ye did it not to me.** And these shall go away into everlasting punishment: but the righteous into life eternal. (Matthew 25:31-46)

There are no merits attributable to us by our works. The righteousness of Christ is imputed to us.

Not by works of righteousness which we have done, but according to his mercy he saved us, by the washing of regeneration, and renewing of the Holy Ghost. (Titus 3:5)

The works spoken of by James are the works of Christ and not our works.

Who hath saved us, and called us with an holy calling, not according to our works, but according to his own purpose and grace, which was given us in Christ Jesus before the world began. (2 Timothy 1:9)

It is the very works spoken of by James that are the fruit of the saving faith of Jesus and worked out by Jesus through those that God sees at the judgment seat of Christ. That is, Christ sees his own good works performed through his elect. The Bible states that it is God that works through the believer.

> Wherefore, my beloved, as ye have always obeyed, not as in my presence only, but now much more in my absence, work out your own salvation with fear and trembling. **For it is God which worketh in you both to will and to do of his good pleasure.** (Philippians 2:12-13)

There is no merit gained to the believer and no reward that they can claim as something they merit. Jesus Christ has done it all. Notice what Jesus says; he does not say come and receive your reward. Instead, he announces: **"inherit the kingdom prepared for you from the foundation of the world**." An inheritance is not earned for something well done; it is bestowed for who you are. You are an elect child of God, saved for eternity by his grace through faith in Jesus Christ.

Christians who appear before the throne of Christ, will find it to be a throne of mercy, not judgment. "Let us therefore come boldly unto **the throne of grace**, that we may obtain mercy, and find grace to help in time of need." (Hebrews 4:16) How could the judgment seat of Christ be a throne of grace if God will judge all (saved and unsaved) according to their works, and the Bible makes it clear that we cannot be saved by works? The answer is found in the Bible. In Ephesians 2:8-10, God states that Christians are saved by his grace through faith in Jesus Christ and are pre-ordained to be born again and walk in good works. God's elect are spiritual creations of God for the purpose of walking in good works. Those good works are prepared by God in advance for us to perform.

If his will is that we will do good works, then we will do good works; his will is done on earth just as his will is done in heaven. "Thy kingdom come. **Thy will be done in earth, as it is in heaven**." (Matthew 6:10) God acts in accordance with his will, and no one can stay the hand of God!

> And all the inhabitants of the earth are reputed as nothing: and **he doeth according to his will in the army of heaven, and among the inhabitants of the earth: and none can stay his hand**, or say unto him, What doest thou? (Daniel 4:35)

Notice in Matthew 25:31-46 on judgment day, Jesus only sees the good works of the sheep (saved Christians) and he only sees the bad works of the goats (unsaved heathen). Why is that? Because Jesus works through the saved sheep to do good works; aside from Jesus no man can do any good. "Even so every good tree bringeth forth good fruit; but a corrupt tree bringeth forth evil fruit. **A good tree cannot bring forth evil fruit, neither can a corrupt tree bring forth good fruit.** Every tree that bringeth not forth good fruit is hewn down, and cast into the fire." (Matthew 7:17-19)

God will not consider or recompense any sins committed by his sheep. All the sins of his sheep have been forgiven and washed clean in the blood of the lamb of God. Revelations 7:14. God has stated that he will completely forgive and even forget the sins of his elect. "For I will be merciful to their unrighteousness, and their sins and their iniquities will I remember no more." (Hebrews 8:12) Though the sins be crimson red God will so cleanse the sinner that they shall be white as snow. Isaiah 1:18. Christ has reconciled God to his elect sheep and no sins will be imputed to them. When God looks upon his sheep, he only sees the righteous acts done by Christ through them.

Only those who are in Jesus will have any good works on judgment day because those good works are actually the works of Christ performed through them. "The steps of a good man are ordered by the Lord: and he delighteth in his way." Psalm 37:23. A man may think that he is ordering his own steps, but he is not. "O LORD, I know that the way of man is not in himself: it is not in man that walketh to direct his steps." (Jeremiah 10:23) God is directing the steps of men. "A man's heart deviseth his way: but the Lord directeth his steps." Proverbs 16:9.

Without Jesus, a person can do no good works by God's standard. "I am the vine, ye are the branches: **He that abideth in me, and I in him, the same bringeth forth much fruit: for without me ye can do nothing**." (John 15:5) All those who are saved will bear fruit. The very idea that his children will not bear fruit contradicts the word of God. Just as without Christ no man can bear fruit, so also with Christ no man can be fruitless.

In 1 Corinthians 15:10, Paul confirms that without Christ he cannot bring forth fruit from his labor. His labor bore abundant fruit not by his own merit, but rather by God's grace.

> But by the grace of God I am what I am: and his grace which was bestowed upon me was not in vain; but I laboured more abundantly than they all: **yet not I, but the grace of God which was with me.** (1 Corinthians 15:10)

What are the fruits of salvation bestowed upon us by Christ? They include faith, virtue, knowledge, temperance, patience, godliness, brotherly kindness, and charity.

> And beside this, giving all diligence, add to your faith virtue; and to virtue knowledge; And to knowledge temperance; and to temperance patience; and to patience godliness; And to godliness brotherly kindness; and to brotherly kindness charity. For if these things be in you, and abound, they make you that ye shall neither be

barren nor unfruitful in the knowledge of our Lord Jesus Christ. (2 Peter 1:5-8)

In Matthew 25 Jesus tells his sheep "inherit the kingdom prepared for you from the foundation of the world." He has made all Christians to inherit his kingdom. We are God's children and his heirs. "And hath made us kings and priests unto God and his Father; to him be glory and dominion for ever and ever. Amen." (Re 1:6) What blessing is he going to withhold from his children? "But as it is written, Eye hath not seen, nor ear heard, neither have entered into the heart of man, the things which God hath prepared for them that love him." (1Co 2:9)

Notice also in Revelation 20 the great and small stand before God and there are "books"that are opened. One of the books is the book of life. The dead are judged according to what was in the books. Only those that are not found in the book of life were cast into the lake of fire. Just as in Matthew 25 all are judged according to their works.

> And I saw a great white throne, and him that sat on it, from whose face the earth and the heaven fled away; and there was found no place for them. And I saw the dead, small and great, stand before God; **and the books were opened: and another book was opened, which is the book of life: and the dead were judged out of those things which were written in the books, according to their works.** And the sea gave up the dead which were in it; and death and hell delivered up the dead which were in them: **and they were judged every man according to their works.** And death and hell were cast into the lake of fire. This is the second death. And **whosoever was not found written in the book of life was cast into the lake of fire.** (Revelation 20:11-15)

Only those that are saved have done any good works, and they are the only ones found in the book of life. "And there shall in no wise enter into it any thing that defileth, neither whatsoever worketh abomination, or maketh a lie: but **they which are written in the Lamb's book of life.**" (Revelation 21:27)

So we see from Matthew 25 that in 2 Corinthians 5:10 when <u>all</u> appear at the judgment seat of Christ, those who receive according to the <u>good</u> they have done are saved Christians (<u>sheep</u> on his right hand) and those who receive the <u>bad</u> are unsaved heathen (<u>goats</u> on his left hand). "For we must all appear before the judgment seat of Christ; that every one may receive the things done in his body, according to that he hath done, whether it be good or bad." (2 Corinthians 5:10) Indeed, Paul explains:

> Who will render to every man according to his deeds: To them who by patient continuance in well doing seek for glory and honour and immortality, eternal life: But unto them that are contentious, and do not obey the truth, but obey unrighteousness, indignation and wrath. (Romans 2:6-8)

Without Jesus Christ, a person is unsaved and can do no good. John 15:5. All the supposed good and righteous works of the heathen are worthless to the Lord. "But we are all as an unclean thing, and **all our righteousnesses are as filthy rags**; and we all do fade as a leaf; and our iniquities, like the wind, have taken us away." (Isaiah 64:6)

With Jesus Christ, a Christian bears much fruit and God sees no bad in him and forgets all his sins: "**For I will be merciful to their unrighteousness, and their sins and their iniquities will I remember no more**." (Hebrews 8:12)

There is no "in-between" where God sees the good and bad of Christians and the good and bad of the unbelieving heathen. It is all or nothing with God. One is either perfectly holy in his kingdom by the imputed righteousness of Christ or he is evil according to man's fallen nature. With regard to the unregenerate man, God's view is: "They are all gone out of the way, they are together become unprofitable; **there is none that doeth good, no, not one**." (Romans 3:12)   However, the believer is "justified:" "For all have sinned, and come short of the glory of God; **Being justified freely by his grace** through the redemption that is in Christ Jesus:" (Romans 3:23-24)

Works are a manifestation of our salvation; they do not earn salvation nor any rewards. Any Christian who relies on rewards in heaven for his works on earth has abandoned God's grace and instead is looking for God to pay a debt instead of relying on the mercy of God. "Now to him that worketh is the **reward not reckoned of grace, but of debt**. But to him that **worketh not, but believeth** on him that justifieth the ungodly, his **faith is counted for righteousness**." (Romans 4:4-5)

Romans 4:4-5 is clear. There can be no mixing of grace and reward. There can be no grace if there is a reward.

When Jesus saved us, he made us to be zealous to do good works. "Who gave himself for us, that he might redeem us from all iniquity, and purify unto himself a peculiar people, **zealous of good works**." (Titus 2:14) Good works flow from the zeal given to us by Christ. Good works are not to earn salvation or rewards in heaven. They are the fruits of salvation ordained by God. Read Titus 3:4-8, and you will see that we are saved not according to our works of righteousness but rather according to God's mercy. Read verse 8, where Paul explains that Christians should be careful to do good works. Why? Not to gain rewards in heaven, but rather because they are "good and profitable unto men."

> But after that the kindness and love of God our Saviour toward man appeared, **Not by works of**

> **righteousness which we have done, but according to his mercy he saved us**, by the washing of regeneration, and renewing of the Holy Ghost; Which he shed on us abundantly through Jesus Christ our Saviour; That being justified by his grace, we should be made heirs according to the hope of eternal life. This is a faithful saying, and these things **I will that thou affirm constantly, that they which have believed in God might be careful to maintain good works. These things are good and profitable unto men.** (Titus 3:4-8)

In the parable of the penny paid to workers, Jesus made it clear that our heavenly blessings are based on God's perfect grace. Jesus ends the parable by explaining that the first shall be last and the last shall be first. One way for that to be the case is if everyone is treated equally, regardless of the order of finish. That is, when all are treated equally, the first will be treated the same as the last and the last will be treated the same as the first. They would be treated the same, and the order of finish is irrelevant. That is illustrated by the fact that all workers received one penny, even though some worked longer than others. Jesus ends the parable by explaining that many are called, but few are chosen. God does the choosing, and all who are chosen receive the same perfect inheritance.

> For the kingdom of heaven is like unto a man that is an householder, which went out early in the morning to hire labourers into his vineyard. And when he had agreed with the labourers for a penny a day, he sent them into his vineyard. And he went out about the third hour, and saw others standing idle in the marketplace, And said unto them; Go ye also into the vineyard, and whatsoever is right I will give you. And they went their way. Again he went out about the sixth and ninth hour, and did

likewise. And about the eleventh hour he went out, and found others standing idle, and saith unto them, Why stand ye here all the day idle? They say unto him, Because no man hath hired us. He saith unto them, Go ye also into the vineyard; and whatsoever is right, that shall ye receive. So when even was come, the lord of the vineyard saith unto his steward, Call the labourers, and give them their hire, beginning from the last unto the first. And when they came that were hired about the eleventh hour, they received every man a penny. But when the first came, they supposed that they should have received more; and they likewise received every man a penny. And when they had received it, they murmured against the goodman of the house, Saying, These last have wrought but one hour, and thou hast made them equal unto us, which have borne the burden and heat of the day. But he answered one of them, and said, Friend, I do thee no wrong: didst not thou agree with me for a penny? Take that thine is, and go thy way: I will give unto this last, even as unto thee. **Is it not lawful for me to do what I will with mine own? Is thine eye evil, because I am good? So the last shall be first, and the first last: for many be called, but few chosen.** (Matthew 20:1-16)

As explained in Ephesians 2, whatever good we do is done through us by God who who preordained our salvation and the fruit of our salvation. We have no reason to boast, and there is no eternal reward for any of our good works because our salvation is not by works but by the grace of God. Even our very faith is from God. Jesus is the author and finisher of our faith. Hebrews 12:2. Indeed, that is why is faith is repeatedly described in the Bible as the **faith "of" Jesus Christ**.

Romans 3:22   Even the righteousness of God which is by **faith of Jesus Christ** unto all and upon all them that believe: for there is no difference.

Galatians 2:16:   Knowing that a man is not justified by the works of the law, but by the **faith of Jesus Christ**, even we have **believed in Jesus Christ**, that we might be justified by the **faith of Christ**, and not by the works of the law: for by the works of the law shall no flesh be justified.

Galatians 2:20:   I am crucified with Christ: nevertheless I live; yet not I, but Christ liveth in me: and the life which I now live in the flesh I live by the **faith of the Son of God**, who loved me, and gave himself for me.

Galatians 3:22: But the scripture hath concluded all under sin, that the promise by **faith of Jesus Christ** might be **given** to them that believe.

Notice in Galatians 3:22 that it is the faith **"of"** Jesus that is "**given** to them that believe." Galatians 3:22 makes it clear that the Faith is **"given"** to the believer by God.

Philippians 3:9: And be found in him, not having mine own righteousness, which is of the law, but that which is through the **faith of Christ**, the righteousness which is of God by faith.

James 2:1: My brethren, have not the **faith of our Lord Jesus Christ**, the Lord of glory, with respect of persons.

Revelation 14:12 Here is the patience of the saints: here are they that keep the commandments of God, and the **faith of Jesus**.

Jesus is the source of the faith. That is why Paul stated that he had nothing about which to glory. "For though I preach the gospel, I have nothing to glory of: for necessity is laid upon me; yea, woe is unto me, if I preach not the gospel!" 1 Corinthians 9:16. Jesus drove home the point when he stated: "So likewise ye, when ye shall have done all those things which are commanded you, say, We are unprofitable servants: we have done that which was our duty to do." (Luke 17:10)

Consequently, if persons come to the knowledge of Christ and are saved due to the preaching of the gospel, that is due to the work of Christ. There is not some added blessing to be received by the preacher in heaven because the gospel they preached was effectual. The glory for saving the soul goes to God and God alone. "So then neither is he that planteth any thing, neither he that watereth; but God that giveth the increase." (1 Corinthians 3:7)

Our blessing in heaven is not based upon some debt owed to us for works done on earth. Our blessing in heaven is based entirely on the mercy and grace of God. Read again what God states:

> For by grace are ye saved through faith; and that not of yourselves: **it is the gift of God: Not of works**, lest any man should boast. **For we are his workmanship, created in Christ Jesus unto good works, which God hath before ordained that we should walk in them.** (Ephesians 2:8-10)

Endnotes

1. Society of Evangelical Arminians, http://evangelicalarminians.org/ (last visited on November 28, 2011).

2. Micael Horton, Evangelical Arminians, Option or Oxymoron?, November 28, 2011, http://www.reformationonline.com/arminians.htm.

3. Franklin Graham, *Expect Suffering, But Not Forever*, April 27, 2011, Billy Graham Evangelistic Association, http://www.billygraham.org/articlepage.asp?articleid=1162.

4. William W. Birch, On Faith and Repentance, November 19, 2010, citing The Arminian Confession of 1621, trans. and ed. Mark A. Ellis (Eugene, OR: Pickwick Publications, 2005), 76-78, http://thearminian.net/2010/11/19/on-faith-and-repentance/.

5. William W. Birch, On Faith and Repentance, November 19, 2010, citing The Arminian Confession of 1621, trans. and ed. Mark A. Ellis (Eugene, OR: Pickwick Publications, 2005), 76-78, http://thearminian.net/2010/11/19/on-faith-and-repentance/.

6. Shawn Lazar, Justification by Works for Baptists (James 2:14-26), March 1, 2014, https://faithalone.org/grace-in-focus-articles/justification-by-works-for-baptists/.

7. Zane Hodges Obituary, The Dallas Morning News, November 29, 2008,

https://obits.dallasnews.com/obituaries/dallasmorningnews/obituary.aspx?n=zane-c-hodges&pid=120756251. Zane Hodges, https://www.wikiwand.com/en/Zane_C._Hodges (last visited on March 14, 2021).

8. Zane C. Hodges, The Epistle of James, A Shorter Commentary (2010), https://faithalone.org/wp-content/uploads/2019/04/ZaneHodges_James_ShorterCommentary.pdf.

9. Zane C. Hodges, The Epistle of James, A Shorter Commentary, at 30 (2010), https://faithalone.org/wp-content/uploads/2019/04/ZaneHodges_James_ShorterCommentary.pdf.

10. Zane C. Hodges, The Epistle of James, A Shorter Commentary, at 31 (2010), https://faithalone.org/wp-content/uploads/2019/04/ZaneHodges_James_ShorterCommentary.pdf.

11. Zane C. Hodges, The Epistle of James, A Shorter Commentary, at 31 (2010), https://faithalone.org/wp-content/uploads/2019/04/ZaneHodges_James_ShorterCommentary.pdf.

12. Lazar, supra.

13. Lazar, supra.

14. John Gill, Gill's Exposition, at James 2:24, https://biblehub.com/commentaries/gill/james/2.htm (last visited on March 14, 2021).

15. Sermon Jam | Justification by works or faith? John MacArthur, Weleyan Fellowship, September 6, 2014, https://www.youtube.com/watch?v=lbYCzWVvt5c.

16. Don Fortner, Fourfold Justification, https://www.angelfire.com/va/sovereigngrace/fourfoldjustification.html (last visited on March 17, 2021).

17. Pastor Steven Anderson What I Hate about Calvinism, July 22, 2019, https://www.youtube.com/watch?v=3ifZuMnMGpQ.

18. Steven Anderson, The True Meaning Of James 2 - "Faith Without Works Is Dead" - Baptist Sermon Excerpt, King James, July 22, 2019, https://www.youtube.com/watch?v=C3QCpp2J5M0.

19. Jesse Morrell, The Heresy of Pastor Steven Anderson Exposed, September 5, 2018, https://biblicaltruthresources.wordpress.com/2018/09/05/the-heresy-of-pastor-steven-anderson-exposed-beware-of-wolves-in-sheeps-clothing/.

20. Carl Roberts' Heresy of Salvation by Dead Faith, March 10, 2021, https://greatmountainpublishing.com/2021/03/10/carl-roberts-heresy-of-salvation-by-dead-faith/.

21. Dennis Bratcher, *The Five Articles of the Remonstrants (1610)*, http://www.crivoice.org/creedremonstrants.html (last visited on October 13, 2011).

22. Dennis Bratcher, *The Canons of Dordt (1618-1619)*, http://www.crivoice.org/creeddordt.html (last visited on October 13, 2011).

23. E.g., D.A. Waite, *Calvin's Error of Limited Atonement*, http://www.biblebelievers.net/calvinism/kjcalvn4.htm#

Terms_John112 (last visited on November 8, 2011).

24. Tom Ascol, Jack Graham on "The Truth about Grace," Pt. 1, August 1, 2005, Founders Ministry Blog, http://www.founders.org/blog/2005/08/jack-graham-on-truth-about-grace-pt-1.html.

25. Tom Ascol, Jack Graham on "The Truth about Grace," Pt. 1, August 1, 2005, Founders Ministry Blog, http://www.founders.org/blog/2005/08/jack-graham-on-truth-about-grace-pt-1.html.

26. Tom Ascol, Jack Graham on "The Truth about Grace," Pt. 1, August 1, 2005, Founders Ministry Blog, http://www.founders.org/blog/2005/08/jack-graham-on-truth-about-grace-pt-1.html.

27. D.A. Waite, *Calvin's Error of Limited Atonement*, http://www.biblebelievers.net/calvinism/kjcalvn4.htm#Terms_John112 (last visited on November 8, 2011).

28. John Cheeseman, *Another Gospel*, http://www.the-highway.com/angospel_Cheeseman.html (last visited on October 19, 2011).

29. Jim Hendryx, The Unconditional Love of God, http://www.reformationtheology.com/2011/10/the_unconditional_love_of_god.php (last visited on October 26, 2011).

30. Pastor Steven Anderson What I Hate about Calvinism, July 22, 2019, at 26:30, https://www.youtube.com/watch?v=3ifZuMnMGpQ.

31. Dr. Bob Wilkin, Grace Evangelical Society, https://faithalone.org/staff/ (last visited on March 20, 2021.

32. Bob Wilkin, How Wrong Interpretation Can Destroy Assurance, June 12, 2019, https://faithalone.org/blog/how-wrong-interpretation-can-destroy-assurance/.

33. Robert Wilkin, Another View of Faith, https://faithalone.org/wp-content/uploads/2020/06/wilkin.pdf (last visited on March 20, 2021).

34. Robert Wilkin, Another View of Faith, https://faithalone.org/wp-content/uploads/2020/06/wilkin.pdf (last visited on March 20, 2021).

35. Robert Wilkin, Another View of Faith, https://faithalone.org/wp-content/uploads/2020/06/wilkin.pdf (last visited on March 20, 2021).

36. Robert Wilkin, Another View of Faith, https://faithalone.org/wp-content/uploads/2020/06/wilkin.pdf (last visited on March 20, 2021), quoting R. T. Kendall, Once Saved, Always Saved (Chicago: Moody, 1983), 208- 217; see also 171-72.

37. Robert Wilkin, Another View of Faith, https://faithalone.org/wp-content/uploads/2020/06/wilkin.pdf (last visited on March 20, 2021).

38. Robert Wilkin, Another View of Faith, https://faithalone.org/wp-content/uploads/2020/06/wilkin.pdf (last visited on March 20, 2021).

39. Josh Toupos, Easy-Believism: Another False Gospel, https://amos37.com/ebag/ (last visited on March 29, 2021), quoting Art Sadlier, The Purpose Driven Church, November 23, 2016, http://soundthetrumpet.ca/media/?id=3427.

40. Josh Toupos, Easy-Believism: Another False Gospel, https://amos37.com/ebag/ (last visited on March 29, 2021), quoting Art Sadlier, The Purpose Driven Church, November 23, 2016, http://soundthetrumpet.ca/media/?id=3427.

41. Josh Toupos, Easy-Believism: Another False Gospel, https://amos37.com/ebag/ (last visited on March 29, 2021), quoting Art Sadlier, The Purpose Driven Church, November 23, 2016, http://soundthetrumpet.ca/media/?id=3427.

42. Josh Toupos, Easy-Believism: Another False Gospel, https://amos37.com/ebag/ (last visited on March 29, 2021), quoting Art Sadlier, The Purpose Driven Church, November 23, 2016, http://soundthetrumpet.ca/media/?id=3427.

43. John Hendryx, *A Short Response to the Arminian Doctrine of Prevenient Grace*, http://www.monergism.com/thethreshold/articles/onsite/prevenient.html (last visited on October 19, 2011).

44. Kenneth Talbot, Gary W. Crampton, D. James Kennedy, *Calvinism, Hyper-Calvinism, & Arminianism: A Workbook*, at 38 (2007).

45. John Wesley, On Predestination, Sermon 58, http://new.gbgm-umc.org/umhistory/wesley/sermons/58/ (last visited on November 24, 2011).

46. John Wesley, On Predestination, Sermon 58, http://new.gbgm-umc.org/umhistory/wesley/sermons/58/ (last visited on November 24, 2011).

47. Stephen Tomkins, John Wesley, A Biography, at 168 (2003) (emphasis added).

48. Tim Fortner, MATTHEW 25C, November 6, 2014, https://www.timfortner.com/matthew-25c/.

49. George Zeller, The Theology of Zane Hodges and Joseph Dillow, http://www.middletownbiblechurch.org/doctrine/hodges.pdf (last visited on March 20, 2021).

50. George Zeller, The Theology of Zane Hodges and Joseph Dillow, http://www.middletownbiblechurch.org/doctrine/hodges.pdf (last visited on March 20, 2021).

51. George Zeller, The Theology of Zane Hodges and Joseph Dillow, http://www.middletownbiblechurch.org/doctrine/hodges.pdf (last visited on March 20, 2021).

52. George Zeller, The Theology of Zane Hodges and Joseph Dillow, http://www.middletownbiblechurch.org/doctrine/hodges.pdf (last visited on March 20, 2021).

53. George Zeller, The Theology of Zane Hodges and Joseph Dillow, http://www.middletownbiblechurch.org/doctrine/hodges.pdf (last visited on March 20, 2021).

54. John MacArthur, *Believer's Rewards*, Grace to You, July 29, 1973, http://www.gty.org/resources/sermons/1327/Believers-Rewards.

55. CATECHISM OF THE CATHOLIC CHURCH, §§ 1030-1031 (1994).

56. H.A. Ironside, The Judgment-Seat of Christ, http://www.wholesomewords.org/etexts/ironside/care4.

html (last December 26, 2011).

57. Lee Roberson, Some Golden Daybreak (1957), http://www.jesus-is-savior.com/Books,%20Tracts%20&%20Preaching/Printed%20Books/Golden/sgdb-chap_02.htm.

58. James Melton, Judgment Seat of Christ, http://www.av1611.org/jmelton/Judgment.html (last visited on December 26, 2011).

59. Douglas Stauffer, Judgment Seat of Christ, http://www.biblebelievers.com/stauffer/stauffer_judgment-seat.html (last visited on December 26, 2011).

60. Douglas Stauffer, Judgment Seat of Christ, http://www.biblebelievers.com/stauffer/stauffer_judgment-seat.html (last visited on December 26, 2011).

61. Douglas Stauffer, Judgment Seat of Christ, http://www.biblebelievers.com/stauffer/stauffer_judgment-seat.html (last visited on December 26, 2011).

62. Carl Roberts' Heresy of Salvation by Dead Faith, March 10, 2021, https://greatmountainpublishing.com/2021/03/10/carl-roberts-heresy-of-salvation-by-dead-faith/.

63. Zane Hodges, Justification before God Is by Faith Alone, Completely Apart from Works, Romans 3:26, November 3, 2016, https://faithalone.org/blog/justification-before-god-is-by-faith-alone-completely-apart-from-works-romans-326/.

64. Zane Hodges, Justification before God Is by Faith Alone, Completely Apart from Works, Romans 3:26, November 3, 2016,

https://faithalone.org/blog/justification-before-god-is-by-faith-alone-completely-apart-from-works-romans-326/.

65. Zane Hodges, Justification before God Is by Faith Alone, Completely Apart from Works, Romans 3:26, November 3, 2016, https://faithalone.org/blog/justification-before-god-is-by-faith-alone-completely-apart-from-works-romans-326/.

66. Zane Hodges, Justification before God Is by Faith Alone, Completely Apart from Works, Romans 3:26, November 3, 2016, https://faithalone.org/blog/justification-before-god-is-by-faith-alone-completely-apart-from-works-romans-326/.

Other books available from Great Mountain Publishing®

The Sphere of Influence: The Heliocentric Perversion of the Gospel
Edward Hendrie
ISBN: 978-1-943056-06-4

This book is a sequel to *The Greatest Lie on Earth (Expanded Edition): Proof That Our World Is Not a Moving Globe.* It will primarily focus on the infiltration into the church of the superstitious myth of heliocentrism and how that infiltration has served to undermine the gospel. The gospel is the entire Holy Bible, not just some of it. Matthew 4:4. Christian belief is an all or nothing proposition. "All scripture is given by inspiration of God, and is profitable for doctrine, for reproof, for correction, for instruction in righteousness." 2 Timothy 3:16. God's account of his creation is part and parcel of the gospel. A person with genuine faith believes what Jesus said about both heavenly and earthly things. "If I have told you earthly things, and ye believe not, how shall ye believe, if I tell you of heavenly things?" John 3:12. Jesus is God. Jesus created all things in heaven and on earth. See Colossians 1:16-18. God has revealed himself through his creation. "[T]hat which may be known of God is manifest in them; for God hath shewed it unto them. For the invisible things of him from the creation of the world are clearly seen, being understood by the things that are made, even his eternal power and Godhead; so that they are without excuse." Romans 1:19-20. If men have a misunderstanding of God's creation, they will also have a misunderstanding of who God is. If people believe in a creation that does not exist, they consequently also believe in a creator that does not exist. It is essential, therefore, to have an accurate understanding of God's creation. God did not make a movable, spherical earth. If men believe in a heliocentric creation, they will necessarily believe in a heliocentric creator. A heliocentric creation does not exist. So also, a heliocentric creator does not exist. A heliocentric creator is a false god. We have been warned to avoid the preaching of a false gospel, which presents a false Jesus. "For if he that cometh preacheth another Jesus, whom we have not preached, or if ye receive another spirit, which ye have not received, or another gospel, which ye have not accepted, ye might well bear with him." 2 Corinthians 11:4.

The Greatest Lie on Earth
Proof That Our World Is Not a Moving Globe
Edward Hendrie
ISBN-13: 978-1-943056-01-9

This book reveals the mother of all conspiracies. It sets forth biblical proof and irrefutable evidence that will cause the scales to fall from your eyes and reveal that the world you thought existed is a myth. The most universally accepted scientific belief today is that the earth is a globe, spinning on its axis at a speed of approximately 1,000 miles per hour at the equator, while at the same time it is orbiting the sun at approximately 66,600 miles per hour. All of this is happening as the sun, in turn, is supposed to be hurtling through the Milky Way galaxy at approximately 500,000 miles per hour. The Milky Way galaxy, itself, is alleged to be racing through space at a speed ranging from 300,000 to 1,340,000 miles per hour. What most people are not told is that the purported spinning, orbiting, and speeding through space has never been proven. In fact, every scientific experiment that has ever been performed to determine the motion of the earth has proven that the earth is stationary. Yet, textbooks ignore the scientific proof that contradicts the myth of a spinning and orbiting globe. Christian schools have been hoodwinked into teaching heliocentrism, despite the clear teaching in the Bible that the earth is not a sphere and does not move. This book reveals the evil forces behind the heliocentric deception, and why scientists and the Christian churches have gone along with it.

The Greatest Lie on Earth (Expanded Edition)
Proof That Our World Is Not a Moving Globe
Edward Hendrie
ISBN-13: 978-1943056-03-3

This book is an expanded edition of *The Greatest Lie on Earth*. It contains more than 1,000 pages of authoritative evidence with more than 1,300 endnotes that document proof beyond any doubt that the earth is flat and stationary. The book reveals the mother of all conspiracies. It sets forth biblical proof and irrefutable evidence that will cause the scales to fall from your eyes and reveal that the world you thought existed is a myth. The most universally accepted scientific belief today is that the earth is a globe, spinning on its axis at a speed of approximately 1,000 miles per hour at the equator, while at the same time it is orbiting the sun at approximately 66,600 miles per hour. All of this is happening as the sun, in turn, is supposed to be hurtling through the Milky Way galaxy at approximately 500,000 miles per hour. The Milky Way galaxy, itself, is alleged to be racing through space at a speed ranging from 300,000 to 1,340,000 miles per hour. What most people are not told is that the purported spinning, orbiting, and speeding through space has never been proven. In fact, every scientific experiment that has ever been performed to determine the motion of the earth has proven that the earth is stationary. Yet, textbooks ignore the scientific proof that contradicts the myth of a spinning and orbiting globe. Christian schools have been hoodwinked into teaching heliocentrism, despite the clear teaching in the Bible that the earth is not a sphere and does not move. This book reveals the evil forces behind the heliocentric deception, and why scientists and the Christian churches have gone along with it.

Antichrist: The Beast Revealed
Edward Hendrie
ISBN-13: 978-0-9832627-8-7

The antichrist is among us, here and now. This book proves it by comparing the biblical prophecies about the antichrist with the evidence that those prophecies have been fulfilled. This book documents the man of sin's esoteric confession that he is the antichrist. You will learn how the antichrist has changed times and laws as prophesied by Daniel, and how he is today sitting in the temple of God, "shewing himself that he is God," in fulfillment of Paul's prophecy in 2 Thessalonians 2:4. The beast of Revelation has come into the world, "after the working of Satan with all power and signs and lying wonders, and with all deceivableness of unrighteousness," as prophesied in 2 Thessalonians 2:10. The antichrist's adeptness as a hypocrite is the reason for his evil success. Indeed, to be the antichrist, his evil character must be concealed beneath a facade of piety. "And no marvel; for Satan himself is transformed into an angel of light. Therefore it is no great thing if his ministers also be transformed as the ministers of righteousness; whose end shall be according to their works." 2 Corinthians 11:14-15. The key to revealing the identity of the antichrist is to uncover his hypocrisy. Because the hypocrisy of the antichrist is so extreme, those who have been hoodwinked by his religious doctrines will be shocked to learn of it. This book exposes the concealed iniquity of the antichrist and juxtaposes it against his publicly proclaimed false persona of righteousness, thus bringing into clear relief that man of sin, the son of perdition, who is truly a ravening wolf in sheep's clothing, speaking lies in hypocrisy. See Matthew 7:15 and 1 Timothy 4:1-3.

9/11-Enemies Foreign and Domestic
Edward Hendrie
ISBN-13: 978-0983262732

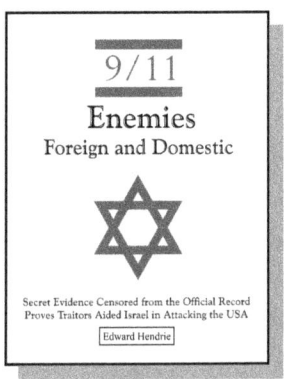

9/11-Enemies Foreign and Domestic proves beyond a reasonable doubt that the U.S. Government's conspiracy theory of the attacks on September 11, 2001, is a preposterous cover story. The evidence in 9/11-Enemies Foreign and Domestic has been suppressed from the official government reports and censored from the mass media. The evidence proves that powerful Zionists ordered the 9/11 attacks, which were perpetrated by Israel's Mossad, aided and abetted by treacherous high officials in the U.S. Government. 9/11-Enemies Foreign and Domestic identifies the traitors by name and details their subversive crimes. There is sufficient evidence in 9/11-Enemies Foreign and Domestic to indict important officials of the U.S. Government for high treason. The reader will understand how the U.S. Government really works and what Sir John Harrington (1561-1612) meant when he said: "Treason doth never prosper: what's the reason? Why if it prosper, none dare call it treason." There are millions of Americans who have taken an oath to defend the U.S. Constitution against all enemies foreign and domestic. The mass media, which is under the control of a disloyal cabal, keeps those patriotic Americans ignorant of the traitors among them. J. Edgar Hoover, former Director of the FBI, explained: "The individual is handicapped by coming face-to-face with a conspiracy so monstrous-he simply cannot believe it exists." 9/11-Enemies Foreign and Domestic erases any doubt about the existence of the monstrous conspiracy described by Hoover and arms the reader with the knowledge required to save our great nation. "My people are destroyed for lack of knowledge." Hosea 4:6.

Solving the Mystery of BABYLON THE GREAT
Edward Hendrie
ISBN-13: 978-0983262701

"Attorney and Christian researcher Edward Hendrie investigates and reveals one of the greatest exposés of all time... . . a book you don't want to miss. Solving the Mystery of Babylon the Great is packed with documentation. Never before have the crypto-Jews who seized the reins of power in Rome been put under such intense scrutiny." Texe Marrs, Power of Prophecy. The evidence presented in this book leads to the ineluctable conclusion that the Roman Catholic Church was established by crypto-Jews as a false "Christian" front for a Judaic/Babylonian religion. That religion is the core of a world conspiracy against man and God. That is not a conspiracy theory based upon speculation, but rather the hard truth based upon authoritative evidence, which is documented in this book. Texe Marrs explains in his foreword to the book: "Who is Mystery Babylon? What is the meaning of the sinister symbols found in these passages? Which city is being described as the 'great city' so full of sin and decadence, and who are its citizens? Why do the woman and beast of Revelation seek the destruction of the holy people, the saints and martyrs of Jesus? What does it all mean for you and me today? Solving the Mystery of Babylon the Great answers these questions and more. Edward Hendrie's discoveries are not based on prejudice but on solid evidence aligned forthrightly with the 'whole counsel of God.' He does not condone nor will he be a part of any project in which Bible verses are taken out of context, or in which scriptures are twisted to mean what they do not say. Again and again you will find that Mr. Hendrie documents his assertions, backing up what he says with historical facts and proofs. Most important is that he buttresses his findings with scriptural understanding. The foundation for his research is sturdy because it is based on the bedrock of God's unshakeable Word."

The Anti-Gospel
Edward Hendrie
ISBN-13: 978-0983262749

Edward Hendrie uses God's word to strip the sheep's clothing from false Christian ministers and expose them as ravening wolves preaching an anti-gospel. The anti-gospel is based on a myth that all men have a will that is free from the bondage of sin to choose whether to believe in Jesus. The Holy Bible, however, states that all men are spiritually dead and cannot believe in Jesus unless they are born again of the Holy Spirit. Ephesians 2:1-7; John 3:3-8. God has chosen his elect to be saved by his grace through faith in Jesus Christ. Ephesians 1:3-9; 2:8-10. God imbues his elect with the faith needed to believe in Jesus. Hebrews 12:2; John 1:12-13. The devil's false gospel contradicts the word of God and reverses the order of things. Under the anti-gospel, instead of a sovereign God choosing his elect, sovereign man decides whether to choose God. The calling of the Lord Jesus Christ is effectual; all who are chosen for salvation will believe in Jesus. John 6:37-44. The anti-gospel has a false Jesus, who only offers the possibility of salvation, with no assurance. The anti-gospel blasphemously makes God out to be a liar by denying the total depravity of man and the sovereign election of God. All who preach that false gospel are under a curse from God. Galatians 1:6-9.

Bloody Zion
Edward Hendrie
ISBN-13: 978-0983262763

Jesus told Pontius Pilate: "My kingdom is not of this world." John 18:36. God has a spiritual Zion that is in a heavenly Jerusalem. Hebrews 12:22; Revelation 21:10. Jesus Christ is the chief corner stone laid by God in Zion. 1 Peter 2:6. Those who believe in Jesus Christ are living stones in the spiritual house of God. 1 Peter 2:5; Ephesians 2:20-22. Believers are in Jesus and Jesus is in believers. John 14:20; 17:20-23. All who are elected by God to believe in Jesus Christ are part of the heavenly Zion, without regard to whether they are Jews or Gentiles. Romans 10:12. Satan is a great adversary of God, who has created his own mystery religions. During the Babylonian captivity (2 Chronicles 36:20), an occult society of Jews replaced God's commands with Satan's Babylonian dogma. Their new religion became Judaism. Jesus explained the corruption of the Judaic religion: "Howbeit in vain do they worship me, teaching for doctrines the commandments of men." Mark 7:7. Jesus revealed the Satanic origin of Judaism when he stated: "Ye are of your father the devil, and the lusts of your father ye will do." John 8:44. Babylonian Judaism remains the religion of the Jews today. Satan has infected many nominal "Christian" denominations with his Babylonian occultism, which has given rise to "Christian" Zionism. "Christian" Zionism advocates a counterfeit, earthly Zion, within which fleshly Jews take primacy over the spiritual church of Jesus Christ. This book exposes "Christian" Zionism as a false gospel and subversive political movement that sustains Israel's war against God and man.

Murder, Rape, and Torture in a Catholic Nunnery
Edward Hendrie
ISBN-13: 978-1-943056-00-2

There has probably not been a person more maligned by the powerful forces of the Roman Catholic Church than Maria Monk. In 1836 she published the famous book, *Awful Disclosures of the Hotel Dieu Nunnery of Montreal*. In that book, she told of murder, rape, and torture behind the walls of the cloistered nunnery. Because the evidence was verifiably true, the Catholic hierarchy found it necessary to fabricate evidence and suborn perjury in an attempt to destroy the credibility of Maria Monk. The Catholic Church has kept up the character assassination of Maria Monk now for over 175 years. Even today, there can be found on the internet websites devoted to libeling Maria Monk. Edward Hendrie has examined the evidence and set it forth for the readers to decide for themselves whether Maria Monk was an impostor, as claimed by the Roman Catholic Church, or whether she was a brave victim. An objective view of the evidence leads to the ineluctable conclusion that Maria Monk told the truth about what happened behind the walls of the Hotel Dieu Nunnery of Montreal. The Roman Catholic Church, which is the most powerful religious and political organization in the world, has engaged in an unceasing campaign of vilification against Maria Monk. Their crusade against Maria Monk, however, can only affect the opinion of the uninformed. It cannot change the evidence. The evidence speaks clearly to those who will look at the case objectively. The evidence reveals that the much maligned Maria Monk was a reliable witness who made awful but accurate disclosures about life in a cloistered nunnery.

What Shall I Do to Inherit Eternal Life?
Edward Hendrie
ISBN-13: 978-0983262770

A certain ruler posed to Jesus the most important question ever asked: "Good Master, what shall I do to inherit eternal life?" (Luke 18:18) The man came to the right person. Jesus is God, and therefore his answer to that question is authoritative. This book examines Jesus' surprising answer and definitively explains how one inherits eternal life. This is a book about God's revelation to man. Except for the Holy Bible, this is the most important book you will ever read.

Rome's Responsibility for the Assassination of Abraham Lincoln, With an Appendix Containing Conversations Between Abraham Lincoln and Charles Chiniquy
Thomas M. Harris
ISBN-13: 978-0983262794

The author of this book, General Thomas Maley Harris, was a medical doctor, who recruited and served as commander of the Tenth West Virginia Volunteers during the Civil War. He rose in rank through meritorious service to become a brigadier general in the Union Army. General Harris established a reputation for faithfulness, industriousness, intelligence, and efficiency. He was noted for his leadership in preparing his troops and leading them in battle. He was brevetted a major general for "gallant conduct in the assault on Petersburg."

After the Civil War, General Harris served one term as a representative in the West Virginia legislature, and was West Virginia's Adjutant General from 1869 to 1870. General Harris was a member of the Military Commission that tried and convicted the conspirators who assassinated President Abraham Lincoln. He had first hand knowledge of the sworn testimony of the witnesses in that trial. This book summarizes the salient evidence brought out during the military trial and adds information from other sources to present before the public the ineluctable conclusion that the assassination of Abraham Lincoln was the work of the Roman Catholic Church. The Roman Catholic Church has been largely successful in suppressing the circulation of this book. This book has never been given a place on bookstore shelves, as it exposed too much for the Roman Catholic hierarchy to tolerate. Any display of this book would bring an instant boycott of the bookstore. It is only now, in the age of the internet, where the marketplace of ideas has been opened wide, that this book can be found by those searching for the truth of who was behind the assassination of Abraham Lincoln.

The above books can be ordered from bookstores and from internet sites, including, but not limited to:

www.antichristconspiracy.com
www.lulu.com
www.911enemies.com
www.mysterybabylonthegreat.net
www.antigospel.com
https://play.google.com
www.barnesandnoble.com
www.amazon.com

Edward Hendrie
edwardhendrie@gmail.com

www.ingramcontent.com/pod-product-compliance
Lightning Source LLC
Chambersburg PA
CBHW051125160426
43195CB00014B/2340